"I ask you, sir, what sort of word is that?

It's "Aooow" and "Garn" that keep her in her place,

Not her wretched clothes, and dirty face."

Professor Henry Higgins
about Eliza Doolittle in *My Fair Lady*

D1417150

"MY FAIR LADY"
(Alan Jay Lerner, Frederick Loewe)
© 1956 by ALAN JAY LERNER & FREDRICK LOEWE (Renewed)
CHAPPELL & CO., Publisher and owner of allied rights throughout the world

Talking *Correctly* for Success

. . . .

A practical guide for business, professional and social success by sounding "right"

James A. Fisher

Avant Publishing Co.

Distributed by
Seven Hills Distributing Co.
Cincinnati, Ohio

Published by
Avant Publishing Co.

L.C. forthcoming
ISBN 0-9625941-0-5

Distributed by
Seven Hills Book Distributors
49 Central Avenue
Cincinnati OH, 45202
(800) 545-2005
FAX (513) 381-0753

Printed in U.S.A.

Foreword

This is not a grammar book, although I have included some comments on grammar just to make sense of some of the irregularities in our language.

Instead of presenting rules of grammar, we simply tell you what *sounds* better.

These issues are always subject to some dispute, but following this guide will put you miles ahead in improving your image. And that's the whole point.

We all learned to speak by *hearing* what our parents and friends said. In the same way, we can relearn to say things in a more acceptable way by saying them, hearing what we have said, and saying them again — by practicing speaking aloud.

Using this guide with a partner will help both of you, enormously more than a solo effort will. A tape recorder will also help. But the most important counsel is to practice saying what is acceptable and impressive, and *hearing* it said.

Good Luck! Have Fun!

J.A.F.

Introduction

We all think of our appearance — "image" is the new "in" word for it — as our physical looks, mannerisms, and much-advised dress. And these certainly are important in our daily work, for sales calls, for example, or for interviews for jobs, for promotions, and social acceptance.

But a good appearance includes good *speaking* habits as well. The nice appearing man or woman — the one who has been smart enough to make mental notes while peering into the correct shop windows — dresses in an entirely proper way: muted colors, natural fabrics, "power ties," sophisticated accessories. But when the conversation begins, a few noticeable mistakes can turn off the interviewer or other listener, and sink the conversation.

The problem lies *not* in any lack of intelligence in the person making the mistake, but in the family, the locale, the schools, and the company he or she keeps. Grammar and pronunciation have received failing grades for decades.

Nothing is gained here by blaming Mom and Dad or Miss Winterwhistle in classes or the childhood chums. The important move here is to become aware of the most obvious, common errors, to *understand* why they are mistakes and what are the correct alternatives, and to <u>sound</u> *better.* That's what this little guide is all about.

You must first become *aware* then *understand* what is correct and acceptable, then *practice* (preferably aloud).

Your achievement will take some work, but the effort will be easier, more effective, and much more enjoyable if it is shared with a partner (we learn to speak by *hearing,* so the sound of the voice is vital). Don't be shy!

And it will all be well worth it, for correct speech can be a winner...or it can ruin an otherwise fine appearance.

And this guide, if you work with it, will make a huge difference...and surprisingly quickly.

A Word on Definitions

There are three descriptive words which appear rather frequently in this guide, and although you probably understand them already, it seems wise to define them here, just to be sure.

Redundancy is the repetition of the meaning of a word or phrase to no worthwhile purpose. We know that *return* means "to go back" so *return back* (often heard) is a dandy example of redundancy and it sounds crude, uneducated. (See the second entry in the guide, **A.M./P.M.**)

A **colloquialism** is a common word or phrase used in very informal speech. The boys from Shipping, gathering after work for a beer, talk up a storm of them. There is nothing "wrong" with them, just as there is nothing "wrong" with blue jeans, but the guide cautions against using them in formal situations, in the office or in business and social life, wherever the words of the speaker are being *noticed.* In short, when the speaker's "image" is on view. (See **ANYMORE**.)

Rural or **hick** is used occasionally, but not in a derogatory sense. It merely indicates that some speakers come from or live in the vast areas of countryside. But business is generally conducted, and success is generally achieved in urban areas where country expressions and pronunciations set a speaker apart as a bit of a character. We simply care about how a speaker *sounds,* and the distinctions made about **colloquialism** apply here, too. Success comes from knowing that everything, speech habits included, has its appropriate place. (See **DESCENT**.)

Following the regular alphabetical list of English words, there is a brief section of foreign words. The reason for the inclusion of this section is explained there.

At the very back of this little book is a "Test Yourself" section. It can't cover everything, but it can be very useful in making the reader conscious of the frequency and variety of possible speech errors. And it's fun!

J.A.F.

About the author...

James A. Fisher is a Phillips Exeter Academy alumnus and an honors graduate of Yale University, where he majored in English. His career in large and small business, industry and consulting includes experience as a laboratory technician, personnel manager, salesman, writer, advertising manager, video producer, sales trainer, editor, executive and marketing consultant, among other professions. He has had a lifelong interest in education and language.

He is the coauthor of a dictionary of teenage slang, and a book on fund-raising for nonprofit organizations.

Acknowledgments

Substantial assistance in creating this guide has been provided by Don Adam, R.L. Hall, Jack Hernstrom, and most importantly by Claire Wapinsky. My thanks to all.

Dedication

For L D

Contents

Part 1
Usage

A/AN

There is confusion as to which is used before certain words. Here is the basic rule: before words beginning with a consonant use **a**; words beginning with the five vowels a, e, i, o and u, use **an**.

If the beginning of the word *sounds* like a vowel, whether or not, use **an** (hour, honor, honest). If "u" has a "yew" sound, use **a** (**a** useful tool).

Also, use **an** before the following alphabet letters standing alone: F, H, L, M, N, R, S and X. That's because these letters, spoken aloud sound like "ef," "el," etc. (Example: "**an** FBI agent.") The "h" is spoken as *aytch*.

Common error: **an** historical event; make that, **a** histori-cal event.

A.M./P.M.

There's obviously nothing jarring about these letters.

What is to be avoided is, as always, redundancy:

- (incorrect) three **A.M.** in the morning
- (correct) three **A.M.**
- (correct) three in the morning

The same is true for its **P.M.** sister phrase.

ABILITY

You (if you want to sound correct) have **ability** *at* drawing but **ability** *with* tools.

ACCEDE/EXCEED

Care is needed in regard to the first syllable of each. The former word means to agree to, to give in. The latter word means to surpass, to go beyond.

ACCESS

This noun means a way in or out (**access** to the fort was by way of a drawbridge). The word is also a verb (to **access** the data or information). A problem arises when the verb use is extended beyond data or other computational usage (to **access** the valve in the cabinet beneath the sink). The extending of the verb use is meant to sound high-tech and impressive, but usually grates on the ear. Try: to reach or use the valve....

Incidentally, it is useful to be sure to pronounce the first syllable "acc" not "ecc" (as in *excess*).

AD HOC

This Latin means toward this or that. It has come to mean: for this particular purpose, as a temporary committee appointed to do a particular job. So you'll sound better not to refer to a *special* or *temporary* **ad hoc** committee.

ADMINISTRATE

Sorry to be the bearer of sad news, but there is no such word. The verb is *administer*. The error has crept in by this route: those who are *administering* are called an *administration* or *administrators*, and there's a fascination with words ending in *ate*. So the non-word was back-formed.

ADVERB

There are three common adverbs that have *two* proper forms.

- (correct) Drive **slow**, move **quick** and go **direct**.

- (correct) Drive **slowly**, move **quickly** and go **directly**.

But it *sounds* a lot better to use the *ly* form.

ADVERSE/AVERSE

Often confused. The former means strongly against, opposed, even hostile. The latter means somewhat reluctant or inclined not to be in favor of.

AFFECT/EFFECT

The former is mostly a verb (rarely a noun); it means to

influence or to produce some change.

- He was soon **affected** by the sleeping medicine and fell asleep.

Effect is both. As a noun, it means the result; as a verb it means to make possible or to bring about.

- The **effect** of the treatment was a quick recovery by the patient.

- His escape was **effected** by (means of) a hack-saw blade and a long rope.

AFRAID

It should be reserved for the meaning of filled with fear. So, "I'm **afraid** that your figures don't quite add up," doesn't really make sense. *Believe* or *feel* or *it appears that* will fill the bill nicely.

AFTERWARD(S)

The meaning is no problem, but it *sounds* much better without the *s*.

AGE/OLD

Avoid the ill-sounding redundancy (repetition of the same thought); don't use both words together.

- (incorrect) The average **age** is 31 years **old**.

- (correct) The average is 31 years of **age**.

- (better) The average **age** is 31 years.

AGGRAVATE

It means to make something or someone *worse*, i.e., more of what existed *before*.

But you can't **aggravate** a situation which is doing just fine. Nor do you **aggravate** grandpa, who is snoozing in the corner. In the latter case, you *bother, irritate* or *annoy* poor grandpa.

AGREE

We **agree** *with* another person; we **agree** *to* a deal, a contract, an obligation to do something.

ALERT

You **alert** someone *to* (not *of*) a danger.

ALL BUT ONE

If you use the phrase just that way, follow it by a singular verb.

- (correct) **All but one** survivor *has* been found.

If you break up the phrase by a plural, then use a plural verb.

- (correct) **All but one** of a dozen rare copies *have* been found.

The same advice applies to *more than one*.

ALL THAT

I didn't like the show **all that** much. What in the world is *all* doing in that sentence? Answer: nothing, so get rid of it.

While you're at it, *that much* is pretty vague. In fact, "I didn't like the show (or ...very much)" says what you mean.

ALLS/ALL'S

The former can crop up in a conversation with a devastating effect, so caution is needed. The word meant, of course, is *all*.

- (incorrect) **Alls** you have to do is send in the form.

- (correct) **All** you have to do is send in the form.

All's, obviously, is the contraction of *all is*.

- Four o'clock and **all's** well.

ALLUDE/ELUDE

The former means to refer to.

- In his talk, he **alluded** to the earlier work of the committee.

The latter means to avoid capture, to escape.

- He managed to **elude** the search party.

ALOUD (OUT LOUD)

The former sounds more refined, less country-boy, better.

ALRIGHT/ALOT

Although this guide generally deals with the spoken

word, we couldn't resist these two-common *written* errors.

Alright doesn't exist, although people are often confused by its similarity to *almost, already*, etc. What you mean to write is *all right*.

Avoid also **alot** (*a lot*).

ALTERNATIVE/ALTERNATE

The former and its adverb, *alternatively*, deal always with choice.

It's *all-TURN-uh-tive* and *ALL-tur-nate*.

- He had no **alternative** but to turn back and retrace his steps.

The adjective **alternate** (and its adverb *alternately*) deals with things which occur in turn, rotating to one then another (a,b,a,b).

There is a noun, same spelling, meaning substitute — a person taking the place of another. Say: *ALL-tur-nit*.

AND/OR

Lawyers love this; it sounds fancy and legal as all get out. In almost every case, **or** will cover the situation. Leave **and/or** for legal documents.

AND or OR

Both words are used to join nouns, but the problem arises as to whether the verb that follows should be singular or plural.

Easy; when **and** is used, the verb is plural.

- (correct) His patience **and** determination *are* obvious to his co-workers.

After **or**, the verb looks to the second (or last in a series) for the guidance as to singular/plural.

- (correct) Bill Smith **or** Tom Wilson *is* going to the meeting.

- (correct) Bill Smith **or** the Thompsons *are* going to attend.

ANY WAYS

There is such a phrase, but caution is needed.

- (correct) Are there **any ways** in which we can help you?

Fine. The problem—and the very wrong impression—comes from the misuse.

- (incorrect) Well, **anyways** (one word), I am going in spite of what he said.

- (correct) Well, **anyway** I am going in spite of what he said.

The sound of the *s* (or lack of it) is very critical in the "appearance" of the speaker.

ANYMORE

If used to mean now or nowadays, at this time, any longer or at present, this is an ugly colloquialism.

- (incorrect) Kids' toys are all made of plastic **anymore**.

Used in a negative sense, there is no problem.

- (correct) Steel *isn't* used **anymore** in the manu-facturing of most kids' toys

ANYWHERE(S)

With the *s*, no such word; avoid it totally. Also avoid *nowheres* and *somewheres*.

APPRAISE/APPRISE (of)

Because of the similarity of sound, and because the latter word is much less familiar, these words are often confused.

To **appraise** is to evaluate, estimate, size up or judge a person or thing or situation.

To **apprise** is to tell, to inform, to cause someone to know.

- He **apprised** them of the disaster.

ARDUOUS/ARDENT

The former means difficult, strenuous, demanding great effort. The latter means expressing warmth of feeling, such as passion or desire.

AREN'T I

Though common, it is a contraction for *are I not* which is obviously incorrect and sounds so. If *am I not* (which is correct) makes you uncomfortable, you have little choice except to rearrange your question to something like: "Is it correct that I'm going?" or "Am I included or not?"

AS

"He's on the same team **as** us." What is really meant is "...same team **as** we are," the *are* being unspoken but understood to be there. Therefore, "**as** us are" is wrong and sounds so. It is "same team **as** we."

AS/AS IF

If you study **like/as/as if/as though** in this guide, you'll learn how not to use *like* to link clauses which both contain verbs.

- (incorrect) Winston tastes good *like* a cigarette should.

- (correct) Winston tastes good **as** a cigarette should.

- (correct) He walks **as if** he had injured his leg.

But the point here is not to over-study *like* and become gun-shy. If no verb follows, **as** is not correct, and the preposition *like* must be used.

- (correct) He swims *like* a fish.

- (correct) Bob looks a lot *like* Harry.

- (correct) Pilots can make judgement errors *like* anyone else.

- (correct) He has a son who looks just *like* him.

So reserve **as** or **as if** or *as though* to introduce a phrase in which the second verb is *stated* or clearly implied.

AS BEING (AS)

There are two common misuses:

First:

- (incorrect) Joe is regarded **as being** the better tennis player.

- (correct) Joe is regarded as the better player.

Second:

- (incorrect) **Being as** the evidence was weak, they offered to settle.

- (correct) Because the evidence was weak, they offered to settle.

AS PER/PER

Used to mean in *accordance with* or *as,* this bit of speech-clutter appears more often in written than in spoken use. But it is to be avoided, if possible (as it usually is).

- (incorrect) **As per** your instructions...

- (correct) **As** instructed...

And *never* use **per** *each*; **per** already means *for each.*

ASK

See **QUESTION**.

ASSURE

It means to convince or make certain, guarantee. Be sure to keep it separate from **insure** (see).

AT

This preposition (like all of its brothers) must be followed by a noun or pronoun. It must *never, never* end a sentence, no matter how often you hear the janitor yell, "Where is it **at**?" to a co-worker.

Practice. Try to think of a period or a question mark *in place of* the **at**.

- He phoned me, but he didn't say where he was (period).

- I can't find Joe; where is he (question mark)?

Silly; but, surprisingly, it works.

Another trick that may be helpful is to imagine the following conversation:

Q. Where's Joe at?

A. Just before the "at".

AVERAGE

When **average** refers to individuals or to parts of a group, it takes a plural verb. (The same is true of *number* and *total*.)

- (incorrect) An **average** of 500 visitors *enters* the museum each day.

- (correct) An **average** of 500 visitors *enter* the museum each day.

But when **average** refers to the group as a *unit*, it takes a singular verb.

- (correct) The **average** is...

AWAKE (verb)

See **WAKE**.

AWHILE

This little guide deals with speech (sounding better), and the difference between **awhile** and **a while** is a written one. But a brief word on a written pitfall will be useful. **Awhile** is an adverb meaning for a short period. Therefore, to say something went on **for awhile**, is wrong, and some hearers or readers will spot it. Say it went on **awhile** or write **for a while** (a noun).

BAD/BADLY

If you had burned your fingertips and shortly thereafter were asked to "feel how soft this velvet is," you might try to oblige, but you would be "feeling **badly**" — that is, your sense of feel would be markedly impaired.

Feel is one of a dozen linking verbs, i.e., verbs that link the following word to the subject of the sentence, and thus must be followed by an adjective. The key is to remember that if the word describes the subject, it must be an adjective; if it describes the verb, it must be an adverb.

- I'm having a chill; I feel **bad**.

- I have a sinus infection, so I smell **badly**.

Other such verbs are: *appear, become, grow, look, remain, seem, sound, taste* and all forms of *to be*.

See also **GOOD/WELL**.

BASICALLY

The original, and useful, meaning (essentially, funda-mentally, pertaining to what is underlying) has been cheapened and diluted by misunderstanding and misuse.

- (correct) The long technical report about the patent is **basically** correct, but it includes a few small references which are incorrect.

- (correct) The large background behind the display was **basically** a wood and wire-mesh frame over which the canvas was stretched.

The other day, we heard one of those brief TV inter-views with a professional football player. Such inter-views are an ideal — in fact unparalleled — spawning ground for solecisms (SOL-uh-sizz-ems i.e., errors).

Responding to a question, the man said, "Well, **basically** I was born in Philadelphia."

Enough said.

BEATEN/BEAT

The past participle is **beaten**, not **beat**.

- The team was **beaten** 35-6.

- Her beef stew can't be **beaten**.

While on this subject, you would do well to be sure that you remember the past participles (form of verb used following *have*) of the 86 verbs which most commonly lead to errors, see page 81.

Get these right; if wrong, they sound awful.

BECAUSE (REASON)

Because means *the reason is that.* Therefore, using both phrases in the same sentence does not make sense.

- (incorrect) The **reason is because** he ran out of money…

- (correct) The **reason is** that he ran out of money…

- (correct) **Because** he ran out of money…

BEHALF OF (IN/ON)

There is a difference here, and the speaker needs to be careful. **On behalf of** means for the benefit of. But **in behalf of** means standing in place of, or as an agent for.

- The lawyer filed a suit against the bus line **on behalf of** all those who had been injured.

- The judge appointed the injured man's brother to appear in court **in his behalf**.

BESIDE(S)

Beside means next to, at the side of; **besides** means in addition. (He is a terrific passer; **besides**, he is a fine quarterback.) Mixing them is a common, colloquial mistake and brands a person as careless.

BETTER/BEST

The former compares *two*; the latter is used in reference to *more* than two.

- Of those two books, this one is **better**.

- Joe is the **best** basketball player on the team.

BETWEEN/AMONG

The former is used in relation to two things or persons.

- John and Pete settled the matter **between** them.

Among is used in relation to three or more persons or things.

- Federal funds are distributed **among** the 50 states.

BI-

The preferred meaning of the prefix **bi** is: occurring once every two of something. Thus, **bimonthly** means every two months, **biweekly** means every two weeks, etc. To avoid ambiguity, when you mean occurring twice within a period of time, use the prefix *semi*.

But this is not true when dealing with *years*. In this case there are two words which you will want to learn to use correctly: **biannual**, which means twice a year, and **biennial**, which means every two years.

See **SEMI**.

BIG (OF)

You do hear — and must be sure to avoid — "It's not that **big of** a problem." The **of** is not needed and wrong. And the sound is very bad.

BOTH

The word *the* never appears before **both**.

- (incorrect) I want *the* **both** of you to know this.

- (correct) I want **both** of you to hear this.

Often **both** is not needed and sounds odd.

- (incorrect) The two reports **both** say the same thing.

- (correct) The two reports say the same thing.

BOUQUET

See **FOREIGN WORDS**.

BOUTIQUE

See **FOREIGN WORDS**.

BRING/TAKE

Which one to use? If the item is away from you, you ask someone to **bring** it closer. If it's close, you ask that he **take** it away.

BROKE/BROKEN

The hint that a reader of this guide would misuse **broke** implies an insult; a sincere apology is herewith extended. Informally it is used (and accepted) to mean out of funds or bankrupt. (He bet heavily, lost, and is **broke**.) It never means shattered or not functioning, i.e., in need of repair; that word is **broken**.

The past tense of the verb *break* is **broke**, and that adds a bit of confusion.

The following are correct:

- Yesterday, his car **broke** down.

- This washing machine, I'm sorry, is **broken**; try that one.

- Your glass vase fell and is **broken**.

- Yesterday, he fell and **broke** a wrist.

See also **PAST PARTICIPLE**.

BUSINESSESE

This is the jargon (made up of part governmentese, part high-tech and part bad grammar) that is tossed around to impress the hearer.

A few samples, and what they mean in clear, correct English follow:

Businessese	English
access (verb)	to gain access to or use of
build down	reduce
bottom line	result, effect or outcome
conceptualize	imagine or conceive
contact (verb)	write, phone or visit
dialog (verb)	talk, discuss
downsize	reduce
downstream	later
envelope (noun)	confines, boundaries

Businessese	English
fall-out	results
feedback	response, reaction or result
finalize	complete (see also **FINALIZE**)
futuring	planning
game plan	plan
impact (verb)	affect
implement	begin, install
in terms of	about or related to
initiate	begin or start
innovate (see)	
input (noun)	ideas, point of view or criticism
input (verb)	put, enter or contribute
interface (noun)	discussion or conference
interface (verb)	confer with or meet with
...ize	put this on a noun and create a "verb"
network (verb)	communicate with others
on board	hired or in the organization
on stream	in operation
opt for	choose or select
orientate (see)	orient, locate or make familiar
parameters	limits
period of time	period
point in time (see)	point (or time)
prioritize	to rank in order of importance
programmatical activity	work (see notes below)
ramp up (verb)	gradually increase

Businessese	English
real time	now, immediately
reference (verb)	to refer to
shortfall	unfavorable difference, deficit
signature (verb)	to sign
so as to	to
state of the art	modern, up to date (We're guessing here; nobody seems certain about its meaning.)
target (verb)	aim for
time frame	period
transitioning	changing
usage	use (noun)
utilize (see)	use (verb)
-wise	there is *always* a better way to say something than to use a word ending in *wise*.

More thoughts on business jargon:

An interactive, cognitive, communicationally oriented, phonic-graphic patterning system for the purpose of manipulating situational, semantic, structural and pragmatic variables so as to facilitate or disfacilitate comprehension.

Meaning? Language!

Can one stand another example?

In the occurrence of an unprogrammed dysfunction situation, appropriate alternate remedial options will be evaluated by relevant engineering personnel prior to

correctivewise action being implemented expeditiously
in the context of a brief time frame.

Translation: if it breaks, the janitor will fix it quickly.

BUT

This simple little word signals several situations where
caution is needed.

In the first situation, **but** is used to mean *only*. Watch
the verb to make sure you are saying what you mean.

- I won't be **but** (only?) a minute.

- I will be **but** (only) a minute (more likely).

The second situation deals with what pronoun to use
after **but**.

Although there are some traditional grammatical
reasons for your choice, you will sound best if you
always use the subjective pronoun (I, we, he, she,
they) *before a verb*. If no verb follows, use the objective form (me, us, him, her, them).

- Nobody **but** *he knows* the secret.

- There was no one there **but** *me*.

The third situation uses **but** incorrectly after *help* or
doubt.

- (incorrect) I couldn't help **but** drop the plate.

- (correct) I couldn't help dropping the plate.

CAN/MAY

It is unfortunate that the distinction is slowly fading
between these two very useful words. But you will
sound 100% better if you use them correctly. The first

means to be able, and the second means to have permission to.

As a museum visitor, you ask the guard, "**Can** I get to the main entrance through this door?" He might well answer, "You **can**, but you **may** not," but he probably would soon be fired, and that would be too bad. The truth is, of course, that the door does lead to the entrance, but is restricted to use by the staff for good reasons, so you are not *permitted*.

You really should be training the kids at home that "please, **may** I eat some cookies?" means *permission*. And, "please, **can** I eat some cookies?" means *do I have the ability* to eat cookies (five minutes before dinner). Of course the kids **can**, but *should* they?

May also has the (unrelated) meaning of *might*. The distinction from *might* is rather slight; **may** is a little more certain, and *might* is a little more uncertain.

CANCEL (OUT)

No need for **out** in almost every use. The **out** is implied in **cancel**; so its use is a redundancy (like *return back*). See **REDUNDANCY**.

CAUSE/ON ACCOUNT OF/DUE TO

If your sentence contains **cause**, you do *not* need, and should *not* use, **on account of** or **due to**.

- (incorrect) The **cause** of his poor marks was **on account of** (or due to) laziness.

- (correct) The **cause** of his poor marks was laziness.

See **ON ACCOUNT OF**.

CLAIM

It sounds better if the use is confined to a right which is legal and just (he **claimed** the prize). But to say, "he **claimed** to know nothing of the theft" is incorrect. Instead try *said, asserted, protested, stated, testified*, etc.

CLASSIC/CLASSICAL

If used in reference to the ancient Greek/Roman times or culture, these two adjectives are interchangeable.

But a 1924 Stutz touring car is a **classic** car.

CLEAN/CLEAR (THROUGH)

Clean sounds a bit like **clear** which is what is meant. But to say **clean** (he stayed **clean** *through* the lecture) sounds awful and is to be avoided.

CLICHE

See **FOREIGN WORDS**.

COMMENTATE

TV and radio use *commentator* and that usage has given rise to this non-word. Say *comment, narrate,* or *describe*, etc.

COMMON/MUTUAL

Common means shared by *many* (our **common** American heritage); **mutual** means shared by *two* persons, such as opinions or experiences.

See **MUTUAL**.

COMPARE WITH/TO

There is an important and useful distinction here.
When you want to look into two things to see wherein
they are alike *and* wherein they are different, use **with**.

- The sales of the store were better, though the
  profits were down, **compared with** the previous
  year.

When you want to indicate the *similarity* of one thing to
another use **to**.

- A microchip can be **compared to** certain nerve
  cells.

COMPRISE

You deserve to know the truth! It means to include,
embrace, contain, consist of, be composed of. That's
all you need to know to avoid a very wrong and silly-
sounding use. In your mind, simply put *include* in place
of **comprise**, and you'll get the idea quickly. Try it!

- (incorrect) Town Council is **comprised** (included)
  of five old fogies.

- (correct) Town Council **comprises** (includes) five
  old fogies.

Thus you now know when not to say **comprise** and
never to say **comprised** *of*. Therefore, the Town
Council is *composed of, made up of, formed of, consti-
tuted of*, etc. The parts make up the whole; the whole
comprises them.

CONSENSUS (OF OPINION)

A **consensus** is the coming together of two or more

points of view or opinions, a general agreement. Hence, **of opinion** is redundant and unnecessary, and it sounds illiterate. See **REDUNDANCY**.

CONTEMPTIBLE/CONTEMPTUOUS

The former is despicable, mean, vile; the latter means scornful, disdainful or feeling contempt (for someone or something).

CONTINUAL/CONTINUOUS

Something which is **continual** is a series of happenings which repeat, over and over.

- We were annoyed by the **continual** ringing of the telephone.

- Since our motel room was near a busy highway, the **continual** noise of the passing cars and trucks meant that we got little sleep.

Continuous means a single thing which is *unbroken* either (a) in time or (b) in space.

- The **continuous** noise from the ventilating machinery was irritating.

- The sandy beach is **continuous** for five miles.

COULD/COULDN'T CARE LESS

The only way to make this overworked (and usually inaccurate) cliche worse, is to get it wrong! Think it through for a minute: you care very little about something; now imagine reducing the amount you care.

Keep reducing the degree to which you are involved until finally you care so little that it is impossible for you to **care less**. Thus you **couldn't care less**.

CREATIVE

This adjective means *having the ability* to create or invent things, productive of ideas, imaginative. We all know such a person.

The misuse comes in the application to the *product* or *solution*; thus a **creative** device and **creative** solution don't work; it's the *creator* (inventor) who is **creative**.

CREDIBLE/CREDITABLE

The former means believable; the later means worthy of some credit or praise, but not extraordinary.

- The child's violin performance was **creditable**, considering her age and the difficulty of the music.

CREDIBLE/CREDULOUS

Careful — both words deal with the "believe" idea. The first one means believable, and its opposite (incredible) means unbelievable. The second word means gullible, inclined to believe too easily, an easy mark.

DEFENSE (VERB)

This is TV, professional football jargon which results in such jarring sentences as, "the Giants can't **defense** against the pass."

When we hear such phrases in business, we brand the user as a jock, a fellow who never grew up after his triumphs on the gridiron. He's the one who argues that

"Zenith Widgets has to **defense** against a hostile takeover."

Upon translation into real English, **defense** becomes *defend*.

Remember, please, it's *dee-FENSE*, not *DEE-fense*.

DIAGNOSED (WITH)

The word is well understood; it's the word(s) that follows which can sound all wrong. For example, John was **diagnosed with** hepatitis sounds very awkward. Far better is *as having* hepatitis. Or, his problem was **diagnosed** *as* leukemia. Or, the doctor **diagnosed** flu. Even simpler and safer: the diagnosis was flu.

DIE OF/FROM

To **die of** sounds far better than **die from.**

DIFFERENT

If there ever was a lazy speech habit (exactly what you wish to avoid), it's the redundant use of **different**. For example: three **different** doctors said he would have a permanent disability.

Three **different** doctors? You mean the three men weren't all the *same* man using disguises?

Obviously, **different** should be omitted altogether, although it's often incorrectly added for emphasis.

Better, of course, would be a *specific* adjective that would enhance understanding, such as three expert doctors or three specialists etc.

Remember that **different** is not *diff-runt*; it's *diff-er-ent*.

DIFFERENT THAN/ FROM

This distinction is without grammatical logic. For purposes of this little guide, however, how it *sounds* is important. **Different from** is correct.

- (incorrect) His answer is **different than** mine.

- (correct) His answer is **different from** mine.

However, **than** is becoming more common and acceptable if the **than** is followed by a clause (containing a verb).

Example: This accident is **different than** the one which *happened* last week.

DILEMMA

You'll want to use this word correctly, and may not do so now. It's a choice between alternatives, *both* of which are unattractive or unfavorable. That's where "*horns of a* **dilemma**" comes from. But a kid in a candy shop, money in his pocket, does *not* have a **dilemma**; he has a difficult, but delightful, decision or choice to make.

DISINTERESTED/UNINTERESTED

They sound very much the same, but there is a world of difference. The former means impartial, not predisposed to either side; the latter means not caring about or not having any concern for.

- A good, fair judge is **disinterested**.

- Careless speakers, are **uninterested** in avoiding the speech errors that cause us to wince.

If you have any trouble with these two, use **disinterested** properly and simply *not interested* for the other non-related use.

DONE

Means finished, accomplished, completed, etc. There *is* a place for this word, when used selectively.

What grates on the ear and nerves is sloppy or lazy use.

We believe that the only suitable use of "are you **done**?" would occur when the cook opens the oven door (revealing a turkey which has been roasting for hours) and puts the question to the bird.

But, please, not when you mean, "Have you finished?" Asking someone, "Are you **done**?" is equivalent to wearing white socks to the office! It sends up the kind of signal you don't want.

Even worse: Have you **done** *eating*?

DOZEN (THE UNIT)

Dozen is singular. "The other **dozen** is here." See also **PLUS**.

DRAPES/CURTAINS/DRAPERIES

Means draperies or curtains. Although this is widely used and basically correct, that doesn't makes it sound one bit less lower class. Best thing is to reserve **drape** to its verb use and to avoid its use as a noun. **Curtain(s)** will almost always do. If you cannot bring yourself to do that, at least use **draperies** (never **drapes**).

DUE TO/ BECAUSE OF/ OWING TO

If there is a clearly identified noun or pronoun *before* the **due to** *to modify*, using **due to** is correct.

- The damage (noun) was **due to** the flood.

If there isn't such a noun or pronoun, use **because of**.

- We started late **because of** (or **owing to**) the pouring rain.

but (to repeat):

- Our lateness (noun) was **due to** the pouring rain.

EACH

This is a v*ery* singular word, so when we get into one of those, "**each** in his/her/our/their way...." keep in mind that the singular pronoun (his, her) is the way to go. If you want or need to avoid the "his or her" doubling-up (to keep everyone happy), you can avoid the problem with something like "we can all help in our own way."

EACH OTHER

When the two words are used together with no word in between, it is better to follow them with a plural.

- Bill and Bob agreed that they would keep in touch regarding **each other's** vacation *plans*.

Each other works best with two people; for three or more people *one another* sounds better.

EAGER/ANXIOUS

The writer is **eager** to clarify this one, but not **anxious** which connotes some degree of apprehension or concern. **Eager** means looking forward with pleasant anticipation.

- He was **eager** to open his present.

- He was **anxious** to receive the results of the hospital lab test.

EASIER/MORE EASILY

The confusion as to which to use can lead to a common and ill-sounding error. Consider: she can operate that machine far **easier** than Betty can.

Adverbs modify verbs and tell *how* something is done (easily, quickly, poorly, etc.). So, the sentence above should use **more easily**.

Adjectives modify nouns and tell us the nature of the noun, *job* (easy, difficult, interesting, time-consuming, dull, etc.).

These are correct:

- She does it **more easily** (how does she do it?).

- This job is **easier** (what kind of job?).

e.g.

This stands for the Latin *exempli gratia* and means *for example*.

So don't say or write, "...for example **e.g.**...."

Also, do not confuse the phrase with *i.e.*, and do not use it in ordinary conversation; *for example* does just fine.

See also **i.e.**.

EITHER...OR

The word **either** is singular. However, if *two* subjects are joined by **either...or**, the verb agrees with the *nearer* of the two. These are correct:

- **Either** he **or** she *is* guilty.

- **Either** they **or** Bob *is* guilty.

- **Either** Bob **or** they *are* guilty.

- **Either** Bob **or** the Smith brothers *are* guilty.

ELICIT/ILLICIT

The former is a verb (to bring out, draw out or call forth); the latter (an adjective) means illegal.

ELSE

"Who else wants to go to dinner?" is easy. But how about:

- (correct) This is someone **else's** book.

- (correct) Who **else's** book was left behind?

- (incorrect) Whose (*possessive*) **else's** book is this?

Add the *'s* to the **else**, not the word before.

END RESULT

Since **result** means the outcome or consequence following some action, it obviously occurs at the *end* of that action. So why the **end**? Redundancies like this clutter up your speech. Try to learn them and weed them out. See also **REDUNDANCY**.

ENORMITY/IMMENSITY

It might appear that the two words mean very nearly the same thing. Not so.

Enormity means outrageousness or wickedness beyond all reason or moral bounds. **Immensity** means the quality of being extremely large, huge.

- The **enormity** of his crime was revealed at the trial.

- The visitors were awed by the **immensity** of the castle.

Note, however, that *enormous* and *enormously* mean the same thing as *immense* and *immensely*.

ENOUGH (OF A)

He was not good **enough of a** manager to run the bigger operation. Please omit the **of a**; they are not necessary and it sounds — and is — wrong.

- (correct) He was not a good **enough** manager to run the bigger operation.

ENTHUSE

A semi-slang word meaning to be enthusiastic about something. You'd be wise to avoid it in ordinary use.

ERROR/ERR

The first word is a noun; it is never a verb.

- (incorrect) John **errored** in calculating the final figure.

- (correct) The baseball team won, even though there were two **errors** made.

What John did was to **err**.

- John **erred** in calculating the final figure.

- You should not **err** in getting these two words straight.

Error has two syllables; say: *AIR-rur*, not *AIR*. **Err** has one; say: *UR* (like *fur*).

EVER

It means always, at any time. It is not needed (and should be dropped) when preceded by *rarely*.

- (incorrect) Billy *rarely* **ever** does any exercise.

- (correct) Billy *rarely* does any exercise.

- (correct) Billy *rarely if* **ever** does any exercise.

It is, however, acceptable to use **ever** after *hardly* or *scarcely*.

EVER/EVERY

Ever means *always* or *constantly*. **Every** means *each and all* excluding no one or no thing. So, caution is needed in the common phrase "**ever** so often" (frequently) and "**every** so often" (occasionally or now and then).

EVERYONE

(Also everybody, anyone, anybody, somebody some-one, nobody, no one.)

These words can, and do, cause a lot of trouble when followed by *his/her/their.*

The common usage problem is: **Everyone** please leave *his/their* coat(s) in the checkroom.

The fact is that all of eight pronouns listed are *singular,* so the sentence should read: **Everyone** should leave *his* coat... We do hear *coats* frequently used (illogically, since each one [individual] has only one coat), and the error goes almost unnoticed.

But what does not go unnoticed is: **Everyone** leave *their* coat...

In that usage, the singular **everyone** and the plural *their* clash and sound jarring. Practice: Did anyone leave *his* hat?

EXACT SAME

A dead "give away" to be avoided, for it will make a very wrong impression. **Same** means that something is a precise duplicate of something else. Hence, the **exact** is redundant and silly sounding; say simply **same** or *duplicate,* or say that something *duplicates* something else (or *replicates* if more than the initial single copy).

EXCEED

See **ACCEDE/EXCEED**.

FARTHER/FURTHER

The words have been used interchangeably for a long time. But the safe way to proceed is to use **farther** in connection with distance, and **further** in a sense of additional or to a greater extent, i.e., more.

FASHION/FASHIONABLE

We all know what this noun means and how to use it.

- She dressed in the height of **fashion**.

- She's always in the latest **fashion**.

- The **fashion** industry is large in New York.

The problem arises when the noun, meaning the current style or mode, is used to describe or modify something that is chic or said to be in style. If an item is indeed in the latest style, then it is **fashionable** not **fashion**.

- (incorrect) She always wears **fashion** clothes.

- (correct) She always wears **fashionable** clothes.

FINALIZE

A non-word. Of all the business/government jargon words, this "word" is the worst. One well known wit said, "I'd rather Simonize my grandmother than **finalize** anything."

It sounds awful, and furthermore, it's unnecessary. Glance at your other choices (all real words):

accomplish	carry through	conclude
achieve	close	consummate
carry out	complete	culminate

decide	finish	realize
determine	fulfill	resolve
effect	implement	terminate
end	put an end to	
execute	put through	…and more.

See also **BUSINESSESE**.

FIRSTLY/LASTLY

In olden days, this (and *secondly, thirdly*, etc.) was correct. But today, forget the *ly*. First, times and taste change; second, what is considered correct changes; third, putting on the *ly* sounds old-fashion, stuffy, and wrong. Same applies to **lastly**.

FLAUNT/FLOUT

Flaunt means to wave something conspicuously or to display it in a very obvious manner. Don't confuse it with **flout** which means to show contempt for, to scorn, or to scoff at.

- She **flaunts** her newly acquired wealth.

- The hellion at school **flouts** most of the rules.

FLOUNDER/FOUNDER

Flounder means to tumble and thrash about in an awkward and helpless way. Think of a fish (perhaps a **flounder**) hauled out and tossed up on a dock.
Founder: to take on water till the boat sinks.

FOOT/FEET

A wee bit confusing. Obviously, **foot** is singular and **feet** is plural, but there's one exception. When **foot** is used after a number (one, two, three, etc.) and before a noun (tape, ladder, street, etc.), it remains **foot** even if the number is two or more.

Otherwise, **feet** is used after the number (two or higher), and no noun follows.

- (correct) He bought a six-**foot** measuring *tape*. (noun)

- (incorrect) He's big — over six **foot** tall. (adjective)

- (correct) He's big—over six **feet** tall. (adjective)

FOR FREE

What you're saying, in a slangy, incorrect, and inelegant way, is *free.* You might use free, for nothing, without charge, without obligation, or (if you're feeling ritzy) gratuitous. Any of these choices is absolutely preferable. Remember *free* means *for nothing.*

FOREIGN WORDS

See separate section.

FORTUNATE/FORTUITOUS

The former means the result of good luck; the later means by chance or by accident (good or bad).

Say: *FOR-chew-nuht.*

Fortuitous is pronounced *for-TOO-uh-tus.*

FORWARD(S)

In almost every case, the word without the *s* is the one meant. The safe, and better sounding, plan is to forget the *s* altogether.

FRANKENSTEIN

The mythical physician and researcher, the product of the pen of Mary Shelly (wife of the poet) in her nineteenth century novel. His experiments created a monster with a criminal brain, who terrorized the local village. Sometimes the monster (unnamed) is mistakenly referred to as **Frankenstein** by those who have never read the book or seen the film.

So if someone has created something terrifying or something getting out of hand, it is a **Frankenstein** *monster* or a **Frankenstein's** *monster*, not the well-meaning but bumbling doctor.

GAUNTLET/GAMUT

The former (pronounced *GAHNT-lett*) is an ordeal in which a person is forced to run between two lines of men who beat him with sticks.

- The prisoner was forced to run the **gauntlet**.

The word (usually *gantlet*) also means a protective glove with a flaring cuff.

Gamut (pronounced *GAM-et*) means the complete range or extent of something.

- The report covered the entire **gamut** of ideas presented.

GENTLER

Means, of course, *more gentle*. This entry is given to remind our readers that the general rule (99% observed) is to use *more* and *most* for the comparative form of a word of *two* or more syllables.

- (incorrect) This medicine is **gentler** to your stomach.

- (correct) The medicine is **more gentle** to your stomach.

Since **gentler** is, unfortunately, heard in TV commercials, we pick this example lest readers gain the impression that it is correct; it is not.

GET/GOT

Overworked, tired, very often unnecessary. It is an insidious word because — although usually not truly incorrect — it weakens your speech and your image.

Consider for a minute: we **get** born, **get** brought up, **get** sent to school, **get** engaged, **get** married. We **get** a job, **get** promoted, **get** fired, **get** divorced, **get** sick, **get** cancer, **get** buried. And there are many more!

Exercise: substitute a better, stronger, more exact word in the this-is-your-life list (you are born, are educated, become engaged, marry, obtain a job, are fired, etc.)

Habit again; what's needed is for us to hear ourselves as others hear us.

GIFT (NOUN)/FREE GIFT

Something donated to someone without there being a payment; something free (no charge). Therefore, **free**

gift is redundant and sounds silly. Did you ever re-ceive a gift that you *paid* for?

To **gift** (as a verb) doesn't exist. A donation is *given*, (not *gifted* … ugh!) to the hospital, church, etc.

GO/GOES

Apologies to many readers, but advice to the few who might err; never use **go/goes** for *say/says/said.* Ex-ample: I show (meaning showed) him the letter and he **goes**, "It's a lie!" and I **go**, "Yeh? Look at the date," and he **goes**, "The hell with that!"

GOOD/WELL

We're almost embarrassed to include what seems to be so obvious an ill-sounding boo-boo, but here goes.

- (correct) She looks **good** in her new dress.

- (correct) He plays the piano very **well**.

GRADUATE

Means (a) to make carefully calculated marks along some measure, such as a yardstick, thermometer, etc., and (b) to promote (someone) out of school or college, with the indication that he, (not *they*: *someone* and *somebody* are singular) has (not *have*) met the require-ments.

- (incorrect) John **graduated** high school.

- (correct) John **graduated** *from* high school.

- (correct) John was **graduated** from high school.

- (correct) The high school **graduated** John.

The student (or thermometer) is **graduated**, not the school. Thus the first example is clearly wrong because John didn't do that to the school.

GREAT

"Bob's now in sales and he's doing **great**." We hear this all too often. We suggest that if Bob is doing well, we'll bet he's not making that error as he talks to prospects. **Great** is an adjective; *how* he is doing requires an adverb (and *greatly* is awkward in this particular usage). Suggest: very well, extremely well or he's very successful, etc.

HANGED/HUNG

Yesterday, the convicted prisoner was **hanged** (not **hung**). But yesterday, the laundry was **hung** out to dry.

HARDLY/SCARCELY

Both these words have a negative sense, so their use in a sentence that is already negative, is incorrect and sounds so.

- (incorrect) They don't have any money or **hardly** (or **scarcely**) any ability to borrow.

You can make this right by saying:

- (correct) They don't have any money and *have* **hardly** any ability to borrow.

HEALTHY/HEALTHFUL

Healthy means sound, well, hale, etc. **Healthful** means conductive to good health (a **healthful** diet). **Healthy** also has a second, not as important meaning of conductive to good health, but it doesn't sound as well as **healthful**.

HELP

Consider:

- He's lazy; he cannot (or can't) **help** but fail.

- He's lazy; he cannot (or can't) **help** failing (or failure).

The first statement contains a double negative (*not, but*) and — though we often hear it spoken — is incorrect. The second statement is correct.

HIM/HE

Normally, no problem (**He** is over there; throw the ball to **him**). But, when *being* is used, sometimes there is confusion, and a wrong-sounding and wrong phrase results.

- (incorrect) **Him**, being an attorney, ought to know the law.

- (correct) **He**, being an attorney, ought to know the law.

He is the subject of *ought*; the *being an attorney* phrase is parenthetical, a sort of added, incidental phrase that conveys a thought, but does not change the grammar.

HIM/HER

Again, we apologize to the high percentage of our readers who will be offended by the inclusion of this too obvious error.

Him (and **her**) never *do* anything or go anywhere, etc. Joe wasn't with us last night; **him** and Cheryl went to the movies. Ouch! It's *he* and *she* who go, do etc.

HISTORIC/HISTORICAL

The difference is slight. The former means important, noteworthy, making (or worthy of) history.

- The passage of the Declaration of Independence by the Congress of the colonies on July 2, 1776 was a **historic** event.

Historical means pertaining to the study of history or the records, results, etc., thereof.

- He wrote a fine **historical** novel about the 18th century French Revolution.

HONE/HOME (VERB)

The first word means to sharpen and, by extension, to improve by practice. The phrase "**home** in" means to steer a course (in a vehicle) or guide a program toward a specific target area or result. Thus, we hear, "we've got to **home** in on that area with all our efforts." Beware of "**hone** in"; the sound of the two words is very similar.

HOPEFULLY

In order to understand the wide-spread misuse of this adverb, it is useful to ponder the meaning of some of its kin.

Truthfully: proceeding with honesty and truth.

Fearfully: in a manner full of fear; timidly.

Just so, **hopefully** means being full of hope.

Here is a good example of the proper use.

- Panting with excitement, the boys dug the sand away from the buried treasure chest. Then Tom, hands trembling, **hopefully** tried the key in the big iron padlock.

You bet Tom was full of hope — and expectations and all the rest.

Here's the wrong use:

- Applications were sent to three colleges, and, **hopefully**, Harvard will accept him.

What/who is full of hope? Applications? Three colleges? Harvard? Why should any of them be filled with hope?

If you substitute *full of hope* in your mind in place of **hopefully**, you'll make few mistakes like the one above.

The correct phrases for which **hopefully** is so often misused are: he hopes, I/we/they hope, one hopes or it is hoped that.

HOSTESS

She's the woman who invites you to her house for dinner, etc. In some restaurants, she greets you at the entrance, welcomes you, and shows you to your table. She is not a stewardess or a flight attendant, and they are not **hostesses**.

HOUSE/HOME

The common confusion and error can be easily solved once it is understood that a **home** is a *place of residence*, a place were someone *lives*, a domicile. A man's **home** may be in a cave, an apartment, a boat, a **house**, etc.

A **house** is generally a free-standing structure usually used as a residence. The best-seller dealing with life in a brothel, entitled *A House Is Not a Home*, makes the clear distinction. A **house** is always a **house**, whether occupied or not. It is a **home** *only* when it's someone's residence.

If a developer builds fifty small separate structures on what used to be a soybean field, and if they are unsold and unoccupied, they are **houses** not **homes**.

Incidentally, the phrase "deserted **home**" makes no sense, since **home** is a place where someone lives.

i.e.

This stands for the Latin *id est* and means *that is*. So don't say or write "...that is, **i.e.** such and such." Just say "...that is." Don't use **i.e.** to mean *for example*; use **e.g.** (see) for that.

I/ME

Oh my, the danger here! This all-too-common confusion gives you away and leaves a very bad impression. Beware.

The problem stems from some myth or fear that **me** is a dirty word; it is not.

Me must be used (a) as the object of a verb, and (b) as the object of a preposition.

- He *punched* **me**.

- He was standing *behind* **me**.

- Just *between* you and **me**...

- Ordinary people *like* you and **me**.

It is never used as the subject of a verb.

- (incorrect) **Me** and Jerry went home.

- (incorrect) Serving you in the forward cabin are Wendy, Cindy, George and **me**, Diane.

- (correct) Serving you in the forward cabin are Wendy, Cindy, George and **I**, Diane.

Me must always be used after a preposition. If there is a long list of names, you'll too often hear someone fall into the trap.

- (incorrect) R.J. wants to meet *with* Charlie, Jane, Bill, Smitty and **I**.

- (correct) R.J. wants to meet *with* Charlie, Jane, Bill, Smitty and **me**.

Not that you'll memorize the preposition list, but so you'll recognize them, the 59 most common ones that apply are:

about	considering	regarding
above	despite	respecting
across	down	round
after	during	save
against	except	since
along	excepting	through
amidst	for	throughout
among	form	till
around	in	to
at	inside	touching
before	into	toward
behind	like	towards
below	of	under
beneath	off	underneath
beside	on	upon
between	onto	via
beyond	out	with
but	outside	within
by	over	without
concerning	past	

I/ME/WE/US

We (*not* **us**) citizens have to vote for Smith for mayor.

For **us** (*not* **we**) voters, it will be a late night before we know the outcome.

When a comparison is being made, *than* and *as* will often be used.

Watch for the case (subjective, objective) at the *beginning* of the comparison, and stay with it. Examples:

- The Will left *them* (objective case) more money than **us** (objective case).

The phrase *it left to* before **us** is omitted but *understood* to be there.

But: Harry and his brother are stronger than **we** (subjective case).

The *are* after **we** is missing but *understood.*

IF

Reference is made here to **if** because its omission can lead to an ill-sounding alternative. For example:

- I asked Joe, did he have a copy of the letter.

Obviously, the speaker actually said, "Joe, do you have..."

But the correct and right-sounding sentence is:

- I asked Joe **if** (or **whether**) he had a copy of the letter.

IMMINENT/EMINENT

The former means about to happen; the latter means high up, superior, such as a high authority in church or government. Thus, **eminent** *domain* means by the rule of a higher authority, namely the government.

IMPACT

Used as a noun, this is a useful word meaning force.

- (correct) The **impact** of the speeding car broke down the wall.

Often, however, it is used when effect or result would much better serve and sound a lot less pseudo high-tech.

- The **impact** of the new law will be that fewer forms will be needed.

  Better:
- The **result** of the new law will be that fewer forms will be needed.

Although the use of **impact** in the example sentence is not incorrect, the use of *result* is perfectly clear and free from the jargon that many people find so jarring.

Worst of all is the use of **impact** as a verb. Keep in mind that its basic meaning is to push together. (An **impacted** wisdom tooth cannot grow straight and is difficult to pull.) Thus when you hear that a report or study is *impacted by* some new data, you should wince; many do. Why take the chance when *affected by* will do just fine. See also **Businessese**.

IMPEACH

It means to bring charges against or accuse. It does not mean to convict.

INEXPLAINABLE

Impossible (or very difficult) to explain; inexplicable. Avoid *unexplainable,* a non-word.

INFER/IMPLY

Help is needed and at hand! These two words are **continually** (not **continuously**) being mixed up.

Infer means to deduce. The trick is to remember the *fer* is from Latin and means to carry (hence *ferry*). Thus you *carry into yourself* a concept or idea:

- I read your technical report, Joe, and I **infer** that you are not happy with the design.

To **imply** is to *express* something indirectly. *You* sort of tuck the idea into the mind of the *listener* or reader by suggestion or other subtle means. In fact, the *ply* is related to the *ply* in *plywood*, the thin layers tucked in between others; both are derived from the Latin word *plicare* which means to fold. The *im* means in. So you fold the thought into the other man's noodle — not directly, but by implication.

So...the writer (or speaker) **implies**; the reader or (listener) **infers**.

Now you know.

INFLAMMABLE/NON-FLAMABLE/FLAMABLE

The first word means readily burnable, but it sounds to some as *non-burnable*, and that presents a possible danger. So, the opposite (by industry agreement for the sake of clarity) is **NON-FLAMMABLE**.

So, if the thing is burnable, it's **flammable**.

ING WORDS

These participles, you'll remember, are those words ending with **ing** (he was *dancing* with his wife). A problem arises when they function like nouns; they then become gerunds.

- **Dancing** can be good exercise.

Here's the catch: you would always say, "that's *my* book," *book* being the noun and *my* modifying it.

But you might use a pronoun to modify a gerund, which *(functioning as a noun)* requires a *possessive* pronoun.

- (incorrect) They started the meeting without *me* **knowing** about it.

- (correct) They started the meeting without *my* **knowing** about it.

While on the subject of **ing** words, try to remember to pronounce the "g" (avoid **dancin'**).

INNOVATE/INNOVATIVE/INNOVATION

The verb **innovate** means to begin or introduce (something new). If intransitive (no object follows), it means to be creative, original or imaginative, etc.

The adjective **innovative** applies to a *person* who possesses such qualities.

The misuse comes when those human qualities are applied to the *product*. The ten-cent, one-second, never-fail can-opener is *not* **innovative**, but the inventor/designer surely *is*. Watch this one.

Innovation can mean either the process of innovating the change, or the new thing introduced.

Perhaps the foggiest use of these words comes in *new* **innovation** (which is only matched by a *new-born, neonatal baby*). See **REDUNDANCY**.

Would you believe that there appeared in a city newspaper a "new **innovation** (introduced) *for the first time*?" *Double* redundancies are rare!

These three words are well worth understanding; they are frequently used incorrectly in the business jargon that today passes for language. **Innovate** a program of clarity! See also **BUSINESSESE**.

INSTEAD OF

This is a prepositional phrase, hence it requires a gerund (word ending *ing*) or noun, to follow.

- (incorrect) He ought to work hard on his studies **instead of** *spend* time loafing.

- (correct) He ought to work hard on his studies **instead of** spending time loafing.

INSURE/ENSURE

They both mean to make certain. However, **insure** has the added meaning of covering by an insurance policy. Therefore, it just sounds better to use **ensure** in talking precautionary and preventive measures.

- He wore heavy clothes to **ensure** his (not him) being warm.

Leave to **insure** the solo job of covering by an insurance policy.

INTO/TO

Be aware that the usual meaning involves (a) containment or (b) collision; it implies a move from outside something to inside the thing.

- No one knew what he put **into** the mysterious mixture.

- He ran **into** a tree.

Therefore, considering how strange it must sound to say, "I'll be flying **into** Chicago."

What is meant, of course, is, "I'll be flying **to** Chicago."

INVOKE/EVOKE

The former means to apply or call upon some authority, law, etc. Watch out for **evoke**, meaning to call forth, reawaken, cause to be brought to mind.

IRREGARDLESS

There is no such word.

- (incorrect) He went ahead **irregardless** of the dangers.

- (correct) He went ahead **regardless** of the dangers.

The confusion arises because of *irredeemable, irregular*, and a dozen more.

Sorry; it's an exception and the error would be enormously obvious in your speech.

IRREVELANT

There is no such word. It has gotten confused with *relevant* (related, pertinent) and its opposite *irrelevant*.

IT/THEY

A corporation, association, company, club, organization or any group organized and functioning as a single unit or entity is singular.

- (incorrect) DuPont is closing **their** old New Jersey plant.

- (correct) DuPont is closing **its** old New Jersey plant.

A recent, regrettable ad for a U.S. auto maker stated that it is "the only American maker (singular) who builds **their** (plural) convertibles."

IT'S

Obviously, this is an abbreviation for *it is* and the danger arises in not following the **it's** by the nominative pronoun (I, we, they, she, he), instead of the *incorrect* me, us, them, her, him.

This will seem awkward and difficult to some, but the discomfort can be avoided by simply using the name (**it's** Bill). But using the wrong pronoun sounds awful, and the fact that the sentence is often very short (**it's** her) makes the error even more apparent.

Turning the sentence around helps in understanding the logic: you would never say "her is it."

Say: "**it's** she," or "**it's** Mary".

IT'S/IT HAS

Dictionaries disagree sharply on this. But your goal is to play it safe and sound correct. So best reserve **it's** for *it is,* not **it has.**

- (correct) **It's** important to speak correctly to make the best impression.

- (incorrect) **It's** been three months since we started.

- (correct) **It has** been three months since we started.

The same idea applies to *here's* which is, obviously, *here is* (not *are*), and *there's* (*there is*).

-IZE

Coining verbs by sticking **-ize** on the end of the nouns has become a national pastime. With a very few exceptions which are very well established (temporize, summarize, harmonize, homogenize, fraternize, ferti-lize), they should be avoided because they make the speaker sound like a kid trying to show off by talking high-tech. They are, for the most part, jarring to the ear. See **FINALIZE** and **BUSINESSESE**.

Same applies to verbs; why *conceptualize* and *moistur-ize* when everyone can so easily grasp *conceive* and *moisten?*

KIND OF

Those **kind of** students just don't care. Right? Obvi-ously wrong! **Kind** is singular and *those* simply won't fit.

Solutions:

- That **kind of** student...

- Students of that **kind**...

The same danger applies to **type** and **sort**. See also **TYPE/STYLE/SORT/KIND OF**.

Avoid using **kind of** to mean *somewhat* or *rather.*

- (incorrect) He became **kind of** discouraged over the work involved.

- (correct) He became *rather or somewhat* discour-aged over the work involved.

KUDOS

The word means honor, praise, renown. The *s* in this Greek word does not signify plural (a *kudo* doesn't exist). Therefore: The **kudos** is well deserved. The plural is spelled and pronounced the same (the **kudos** are…).

LADY

All adult females are *women*, but only some of them are **ladies**. The same concept is true of *men* vs. *gentlemen*. Referring to the woman in the mini-skirt, standing on the street corner at midnight, smiling at men in passing cars as a **lady** is naive and has an unsophisticated quality that doesn't sound right at all. See **WOMAN**.

LATIN SINGULAR/PLURAL

There are some words taken directly from Latin which form their plurals in ways markedly different from the ways usually used in English. Most of our remembrances of Latin are rather rusty, so here goes (plural in parenthesis):

Addendum (addenda): Something that is added.

Agendum (agenda): A thing to be done. If agenda is used to mean a *list* of thing to be done, then a singular verb is used.

Alumnus (alumni): A male graduate. The last syllable of the plural rhymes with *eye*.

Alumna (alumnae): A female graduate. The last syllable of the plural rhymes with *see*.

Bacterium (bacteria): The microorganism that can cause disease.

Curriculum (curricula): The course of studies offered at a school or college.

Criterion (criteria): A standard by which something is judged.

Datum (data): A piece of information — often a number.

These fairly common words are all plural: *indices, errata, media, memoranda, phenomena, strata, graffiti.* The singular: *index, erratum, medium, memorandum, phenomenon, stratum, graffito.*

LATTER

It means the second of two, not the last of three or more.

LAY

See **LIE/LAY**.

LEAVE

Misuse here can be fatal. In the present tense, it means to depart.

- If I **leave** now, I'll just catch the train.

It never means *let* as in the sense of allow. Therefore, it is never "**leave** the poor bird go free." The past tense of **leave** is *left*. It sounds like *let*, but it not the same at all.

- Yesterday, he **left** his office earlier than usual.

See also **LET**.

LESS/FEWER

Very common error and an almost sure give-away!

The rule? Easy! If you can *count* them (one, two, three) use **fewer**. If it's a general, undifferentiable quantity (snow, rain, coal, heat, expense, etc.) use **less**.

- We had **fewer** visitors this summer.

- We had **less** snow this winter.

If it's sales, it can be either; are you speaking of transactions or total dollars? You received **fewer** orders, made **fewer** sales; in general, sales were **less** than the previous season.

LET

It means to allow. Under no circumstances should you confuse it with *left*.

- (incorrect) He opened the cage and *left* the bird go.

- (correct) He opened the cage and **let** the bird go.

- (correct) **Let** *him* (not *he*) with enough courage, go first

LET'S (US)

Remember that **let's** means **let us** so your verb (example: *go*) should follow, not *us*.

- (correct) **Let's** (or **let us**) go!

LIABLE

Legally, it means that you are responsible and can be sued and lose. Hence, when we rather commonly hear, "He's **liable** to change his mind and decline our offer," the speaker is being imprecise and casual. Far better, in that instance, that he say *"he is likely to ..."*

And **liable** is not pronounced *LYE-bul.* It's *LYE-uh-bul.*

LIE/LAY

Oh my, what murdering of the language occurs over these words; how often the listener secretly says "ouch" — and how *noticeable* and *unnecessary* this error is!

The problem arises from a lack of (a) understanding and (b) practice. Look at them in order.

Lie means to rest, recline, stay, remain. It's an intransitive verb; no object can follow it. In other words, you can't **lie** anything.

Unfortunately, the past tense of **lie** is **lay**, which is spelled and pronounced exactly as is another English word with a totally different meaning.

- When you're tired, you **lie** down.

- Yesterday I was tired, so I **lay** on the couch before dinner.

- I have *lain* on the beach all afternoon, and I'm no more tan than I was in the morning.

Now look at **lay** (a different word). It means to place or set (something) in position. There is always an object; the popular ones are eggs, carpets and bricks. There is also a vulgar use involving females.

The past tense is the same as the present, and the past participle is *laid*.

- **Lay** the baskets on the table.

- Yesterday, they **lay** the hall carpet.

- He has *laid* as many as 600 bricks in a day.

The present participle forms of the two verbs are *lying* and *laying*.

- I like *lying* on the beach.

- The hens are *laying* more eggs this spring.

So when you hear, "You look tired; why don't you **lay** down for a while?" you privately groan (or should), but you also have a valuable clue as to how to practice!

The gimmick is that the misuse of **lay** for **lie** is almost always followed by *down*. *Down* is the name of soft, small feathers that are on a duck's, goose's or swan's underbody. You can, therefore, "**lay** *down*" *only* if you have a *supply* of these feathers. Silly? You bet, but a valuable reminder.

LIGHT-YEAR

This is a measure of distance (how far light will travel in a year), *not* time.

LIKE

If you use **like** to mean about, nearly, kind of, or in a way, this is teen trash-talk.

"It was — **like** — two in the morning, and he was — **like** — reeling around and — **like** — singing crazy songs" is as about as wrong-sounding as you can get. See also **YA KNOW**.

LIKE (FOR)

As in, "I'd **like for** you to go to the meeting." This is almost entirely a Southern USA problem, but once in a while it turns up elsewhere — and sounds equally incorrect anywhere. The **for** is simply unnecessary and causes the listener to wince. Say: "I'd **like** you to go…" Same idea applies to *love* (**for**) or *want* (**for**), etc.

LIKE/AS/AS IF/AS THOUGH

It is hard to find an error that has a more devastating effect on a listener than this one.

Like is a preposition; it cannot be used as a conjunction (meaning a word which joins together two clauses, each containing *verbs*). In deciding which word (**like** or **as**) to use, the presence of the *verb* in the *succeeding* clauses is the key. If it's stated (or clearly implied though not stated), you sound far better if you use **as**, **as if** or **as though**.

Some examples (all correct):

- The glider pilot rises and falls with air currents **as** a gull *does* in a good breeze.

- He limped **as if** he *had hurt* his leg.

- The machine ran just **as** it *was supposed* to do.

- He performed **as** well as I *(did)*.

- Paul looks **like** his brother.

- Plastic is **like** hardwood.

- To meet the deadline, Joe worked **like** hell.

- It was a vacation **like** I took last summer (the words *the one* are understood after **like**; it would sound better if they were stated).

So the next time you hear, "**Like** I *say...*" (this will probably be within the next five minutes or less), it will be your turn to wince. "**As** I say..." is not only correct, but *sounds* much better.

A great deal of trouble stems from words like *feel*, *seem* and *look*. Learn to use them as "alarms" for what will follow.

- He *felt* (will a verb follow?) **like** he *was* (verb) under water. The **like** should be **as if**. And, to be totally correct, the *was* should be *were* (see **SUBJUNCTIVE**).

Note: The author well realizes that time changes language, and errors (and mispronunciations) can become, over a long period, accepted and "correct." The word **like** as a conjunction is heard increasingly in speech, as advertising copy writers try to write in the manner of common speech; that increases the (wrong) usage and the cycle feeds on itself. So, it becomes a matter of risk-taking — a personal decision. If you believe that there is no chance that your listener knows the difference, then "...**like** I always say" will cause no reaction at all. If you believe that your listener can tell the difference, and, therefore, could be offended, you will not take the risk, and use "...**as** I always say."

This guide suggests: why take a chance?

LION'S SHARE

Many think — incorrectly — that this means a large share — a very large share. The original expression, however, means the whole lot — everything. Which is what, we are told, lions customarily *do* take of a kill in the wild.

LITERALLY

It **literally** means true to the exact meaning of the *letters* in the words. In short, it means in fact. So be careful to reserve it for those occasions when you mean just that (as opposed to *so to speak*, *figuratively*, *virtually*, etc.).

Here's an example of misuse, the kind you hear every day.

- (incorrect) He was so mad that, **literally**, smoke was coming out of his ears.

Come now! Not really!

LIVID

When Joe was accused, his face became **livid** with embarrassment, anger and rage. Was it? Our guess is that Joe's face was red. **Livid** means lead-colored (ashen, gray, or black and blue).

LOAN/LEND

There is technically nothing wrong with using **loan** (the verb) in place of **lend**. It's part of the recent trend in which nouns creep over into gradual use as verbs. (See also **IMPACT**.)

But we're concerned in this guide as to how it *sounds* – or sounds to a reasonably significant number of listeners.

And "**loan** me your pen," simply sounds as if (not **like**) it is incorrect. Worse — it grates on the educated ear. Why take the chance when **lend** is so safe and handy?

The past tense of **lend** is **lent** (yesterday, he **lent** Joe the money).

MAITRE D'HOTEL

See **FOREIGN WORDS**.

MAJORITY/MOST

While it means the larger number or part of something, it is definitely preferable to confine its use to something that can be *counted*; in short, more than half of the total number.

Thus, the **majority** of those in attendance voted for the plan. But, rain fell on **most** of (not the **majority** of) western Ohio.

MANY

As a noun or pronoun, it is singular in form, though always followed by a plural verb.

- That (not *those*) **many** play (not *plays*) golf on the weekend.

- It's amazing that we would have that (not *those*) **many** people show up!

MEDICATION

Its prime meaning is simply *medicine*, and its over-use is a classic example of the desire today to sound learned or technical. A secondary meaning (the *process* of giving or being given medicine) should be reserved for those special cases.

METHOD/METHODOLOGY

This choice of words is used to illustrate an all too common tendency today to try to make ordinary speech into something more elaborate, fancy and supposedly impressive. Your own ear will pick up similar attempts. (See **USE/UTILIZE**.)

A **method** is a means or manner of proceeding, usually an orderly and systematic one. The ending *-logy* refers to the *study* or *science* of something (geo: earth; geology: earth science). So, **methodology** is not **method** or *manner*, but the *science* or *study* of **methods**. What is almost always meant is **method**.

MILE/MILES AN HOUR/FOOT/FEET

This is a little bit tricky. What is wrong and (worse) sounds very jarring, is the use of the singular **mile** after an obviously plural number.

- (incorrect) He got caught going 65-**mile** an hour.

- (correct) He was caught going 65 **miles** an hour.

The confusion arises because in the *hyphenated* sense there is no *s*.

- (correct) He was in a 25-**mile**-an-hour zone.

This also appears in the use of **foot** and **feet**.

- (incorrect) He is six-foot tall.

- (correct) He has a six-**foot** tape measure.

- (correct) Cut six **feet** of rope from the coil.

MINIMUM/MINIMAL

The first is a noun; the second is an adjective. There is a proper place for each, but don't mix them.

- Bill does the **minimum** that he can get away with.

- Bill makes a **minimal** contribution of effort to the task at hand.

MOOT/MUTE

See **PRONUNCIATION**.

MORE THAN ONE

See **ALL BUT ONE**.

MUTUAL (AGREEMENT)

Since an **agreement** is an accord between the parties involved, it can't be solo. It always involves two or more, and the arrangement is accepted by both (or all). Hence, it is automatically **mutual**. (Ever heard of a non-**mutual agreement**?) See **REDUNDANCY**.

By the way, it's *MYU-choo-al (not MYU-chal)*.

MUTUAL/COMMON

It deals with the *reciprocity* or relationship between two persons or two things. Two long-time collaborators on some project could well build a respect one for the other; they have **mutual** respect.

If each of two men likes trout fishing, then trout fishing is a **common** interest.

See **COMMON**.

MYSELF

Almost all of the frequent misuses of this word are based on cowardice. The speaker is faced with the choice of *I* versus *me* and — being unsure (not being the possessor of this book) — chickens out and uses neither. (See also **I/ME**.)

On airplanes, the flight attendants will repeatedly dodge the issue, they'll say, "Serving you in the main cabin is (meaning *are*) Cheryl, Michele, Ronnie, and **myself**, Christy." Your unspoken reply is, of course, "**Myself** is a passenger, and **myself** resents hearing our language being murdered."

The rule is to reserve **myself** for (a) the obvious and (b) the emphatic. Note that *I* **must** appear in the sentence if **myself** is to be correct.

(a)   *I* cut **myself** with a knife.

(b)   Don't contradict me; *I* saw the accident **myself**!

Other than that, use *I* or *me,* and learn which one is correct and when.

MYTH

The study of **myth** is complicated and academic. For our purposes, helping to avoid spoken errors, we can remember that a **myth** is an imagined story usually about fantastic people and events. The story does contain an important truth, but it didn't actually take place, no matter that it has been repeated over the generations.

Knowing that, you'll see the nonsense in a sentence like:

• Most of the **myths** about Dracula and vampires simply aren't true.

Yes, you guessed it, that is a **REDUNDANCY** (see) — like *false lies.*

NAUSEOUS/NAUSEATED

The first word means foul or evil smelling, having a bad odor, sickening, repulsive, causing nausea.

Now having understood that, do you still want to say, "I'm dizzy and **nauseous**"? You, my friend, are **nauseated**! And, incidentally, **nauseous** has two, not three, syllables. It's not *NAH-zee-us* but *NAH-shus*.

NEEDS (TO BE)

There is a regional, semi-literate colloquialism that goes: The car **needs** washed. What is meant is **needs** washing or — perhaps more common in America — **needs to be** washed.

Avoid this thoughtless colloquialism at all costs.

NEGATIVES

We are not speaking here of truly uneducated (double) negatives such as: I do *not* (or don't) have *none*. Far more subtle is, I *wouldn't* be surprised if we *don't* get rain. What is meant, of course, is that the speaker is expecting rain, and it would be no surprise. (I'd be surprised if we don't get rain.)

NEITHER/NOR/OR

These words can be a bit tricky.

Consider: **neither** Bill **nor** Bob (was) (were) at the meeting. The answer is *was.*

If the second word is plural, the plural verb sounds better.

- **Neither** the book **nor** the tapes *were* destroyed.

The word **nor** follows **neither**; this is preferred over **or**, though some dictionaries disagree.

But **or** follows *not* (or other negative word).

- He will *not* be distracted **or** quit.

Finally, **neither** is negative in sense, so avoid a double negative.

- (incorrrect) That is certainly *not* the manner in which **neither** boy should act.

NET RESULT/FINAL OUTCOME

The **result** is the outcome of some procedure, after everything has had its effect or has been taken into consideration. Therefore, it is **net** of all the result. Hence, the **net** is redundant and sounds silly.

Same applies to **final outcome**; a true **outcome** is the last thing, so, by definition, it's **final**.

See **REDUNDANCY**.

NOBODY

This, and many words like it (*anybody, anyone, everybody, everyone, no one, somebody, someone*), are singular and take a singular verb and following pronoun.

- (incorrect) These days, **nobody** pays enough attention to *their* speech.

- (correct) These days, **nobody** pays enough attention to *his (or her)* speech (*her* if referring to an all female group).

NONE IS/ARE

This one is almost always a problem. Although **none** is derived from *no one* (which is singular), the **none** does not *always* mean *no one;* sometimes it can mean *not any.*

Common sense is required. If the sense is *not any*, the flavor will be in the direction of plural. These are correct:

- **None** of the coaches, trainers or players **are** under investigation. (The sense is *not any.*)

- All four candidates for the position have good grades at college, but **none is** experienced. (The sense is *no one* or *not one.*)

NOT ONLY

See **ONLY**.

NOTATE

No such word. The verb is *note.*

NOUNSPEAK

It is all too common, and incorrect, strictly speaking, to use nouns indiscriminately as if they were verbs. This happens frequently in business, as the following awful examples demonstrate.

- He **referenced** (made reference to) the earlier report.

- They plan **to office** (to establish an office) in a new building.

- The firm offered **to messenger** (to send) the forms to me.

- We will **target** (aim for) the 15th of June.

- We should be able **to productize** (to turn out) some products by early fall.

- The new brochure will **showcase** (exhibit) the latest models.

- The market is **transitioning** (undergoing a transition) into a new phase.

- The workstation here can **access** (gain access to, address) the memory in the main computer.

- Bob said he needed to **dialog** (have a dialog) with the Division Manager.

- The new law will **impact** (have an affect on) the project.

NOWHERE NEAR

Meaning not nearly; we hear it all too frequently. It jars a fair number of ears, and it's best to avoid this one, and never **nowheres**.

NOWHERES/NO WAYS

As in "**nowheres** to go." These are non-words. What is meant is **nowhere** and **no way**.

Obviously, *ways* is a word. But in "he had **no ways** to go," you have a simple and atrocious-sounding error. **No** *way* is meant.

"**Where's** the phone book?" is fine; it's a contraction for *where is*.

NUMBER

In deciding which verb to use after **number**, you'd be wise to think as to whether the *sense* of the word is plural or singular. In most cases *a* signals plural, and *the* signals singular. These are correct:

- *A* **number** (several) of petitions *were* filed for the upcoming election.

- *The* **number** (amount) who try it and fail *is* discouraging.

OCCURS/HAPPENS

Just as the omission of **that** (see) from a sentence can cause it to sound unclear, so can the omission of one of these verbs.

- (incorrect) An explosion is when a material such as dynamite is ignited.

- (correct) An explosion **occurs** (or **happens**) when a material such as dynamite is ignited. See also **THAT(ALL)**.

OF

We speak here of a not needed and offending **OF**.

- (incorrect) He didn't have enough **of** money.

- (correct) He didn't have enough money.

- (incorrect) It wasn't that bad **of** a day.

- (correct) It wasn't that bad a day.

OF/HAVE

Because the word is pronounced *ov* (as in *oven*), it can be confused with **have**. That's a deadly sounding error, usually occurring after *could, should* or *would.*

- (incorrect) He could **of** made a lot of money.

- (correct) He could **have** made a lot of money.

OFF (OF)

Never. The word **of** never follows **off**.

- (incorrect) He couldn't take his eyes **off of** her.

- (correct) He couldn't take his eyes **off** her.

OK?

OK means all right, fine or satisfactory; but you need to be careful that you use it correctly.

It is too commonly used to fill the gap in the speaker's thinking — giving him a moment to come up with what's to be said next. From there, it too easily becomes a teenager's annoying habit.

"So the car is sitting here out of gas — **OK**? — we're standing there in the rain, trying to wave down a car that's going by — **OK**? — and along comes these cops with flashing lights — **OK**?"

The speaker is, in effect, asking at each step if you understand. If the story is extremely simple, and you do understand, then the result is insulting to the listener.

Worst of all is the use of **OK**, meaning "is it all right with you," when what one is being told has *no* chance of being satisfactory! The airlines are masters of this: the agent at the desk who says to you, "Your flight has been cancelled. **OK**? The next flight is at 2:40 a.m. **OK**? That flight is full, but you're on the waiting list. **OK**?" is not only annoying but invites you to reply, "Hell, no!"

In the case of the unconscious bad speech habits like this, it's important to try to *hear yourself* so as to help avoid these tell-tale errors.

ON

Never, never use **on** to mean in his possession.

- (incorrect) He had only a couple of dollars **on** him.

- (correct) He had only a few dollars **with** him.

Another caution: He held the rope firmly, but it slipped **on** him. The *on him* is unneeded and sounds crude.

The misuse of this word is ugly and wrong.

ON ACCOUNT OF

It is perfectly all right to use this as long as you under-stand that it means *because of*. As a test you can substitute the phrase *because of* for **on account of** in your sentence. And a *noun* must follow.

- (incorrect) The concert was cancelled **on account of** (*because of*) he became ill.

- (correct) The concert was cancelled **on account of** (or *because of*) his *illness*.

See **CAUSE/ON ACCOUNT OF/DUE TO**.

ONE (also NO ONE)

Please remember that **one** is singular (*very* singular). So, this is wrong: **One** should not keep that information to *themselves* (plural). It obviously should be *himself* (or *herself*).

Also: (correct) **No one** should keep that to *himself*.

ONE (OF SEVERAL)

Choose: Are you **one** of those readers who (writes) (write) letters to the editor?

Don't confuse this **one** with the **one** in "Did anyone leave his hat?" In that question, **one** and *his* are clearly singular.

But, turn the earlier question around: "Many readers *write* (correct) letters — are you **one** of them?"

ONE ANOTHER

See **EACH**.

ONE OR MORE

At your place (is) (are) **one or more** tickets for the event. The correct choice is *are* because **one or more** really means some or a few.

ONLY

One otherwise deadly serious writer (on the subject of clear and correct speech) called the problem the "lonely **only**." He meant that very often — because the speaker or writer simply didn't know or didn't remember — the **only** will be *misplaced*. The rule for clarity is a simple one: always put the **only** *immediately before* the word it modifies. Usually this means *later* in the sentence.

Some automobile agencies sell cars or trucks and also rent them. Some do one; some do the other. So if you walk in and inquire, you might be told, "We **only** rent trucks." Does it mean that they don't *sell* trucks? Or did the man mean to say, "We rent **only** trucks"?

How about, "I **only** thought that the first day of the conference went badly"?

Did you **only** *think* rather than *speak?* Or did you mean that "**only** the first day" was poor? If so, say so.

Here's a useful gimmick to train your thinking about the importance of the position of **only**. Consider the sentence:

- I hit him in the eye yesterday.

Counting the position before the *I* and after *yesterday*, there are eight possible positions. Try putting **only**, one place at a time, into each of these eight. See the meaning change?

In many cases, *merely* should follow the same rules: *immediately* ahead of the modified word. Usually this means later in the sentence than habit places it.

The phrase **not only** demands the same careful placement as **only**.

OPTIMUM/OPTIMAL

Optimum is the condition, the state of being, which is most favorable for something. It is a noun.

- The **optimum** for the economy shows supply balancing demand.

Optimal is an adjective. It modifies a noun, telling us that something is at its best.

- The **optimal** production rate made the most efficient use of both labor and materials.

OR

For the most part, words connected with **or** take a singular verb. Sometimes, the **or** is implied.

- John **(or)**, his assistant **or** his secretary *answers* the phone.

When one subject is singular and one plural, the verb generally agrees with the nearer subject.

ORIENTATE

It's a non-word; the verb is *orient*.

See also **BUSINESSESE**.

OTHER/OTHERS

Notice the necessary (and correct) *s* on **other** in this: Of the three features of our machine, no one is more important than the **others** (there are a total of three).

OUT LOUD

See **ALOUD**.

OUT OF/IN

This phrase used to be confined to horse breeding.

- Count Fleet, sired by Golden Boy **out of** Dancing Lady…

Then professional football announcers somehow picked up the idea. In a football sense, a player is said to be **out of** an institution.

- Darryl Jones is **out of** East Mississippi State.

But when we speak of a firm being **out of** Chicago, we are really talking in reverse, for the firm is based **in** Chicago. So unless you are either a horse breeder or an announcer, you're better off saying *in* or *of*.

- (incorrect) XYZ Corporation **out of** Chicago…

- (correct) XYZ Corporation **in** Chicago…

- (correct) XYZ Corporation **of** Chicago…

OUTRAGED/OUTRAGEOUS

The former means to be grossly offended or angered:

- The mindless vandalism of the classroom **outraged** the teacher.

The latter means grossly offensive, heinous, immoral, disgraceful, violent or extravagant:

- The vandalism was **outrageous**.

- The $100 scalper's price was **outrageous**.

If you are *very* angry because of some event, you are **outraged,** but probably not **outrageous**.

OVER

See **WITH**.

OVER/MORE THAN

To say (speaking of age), "Joe is over 50" is fine. But with all other figures, *more than* is preferred and sounds better.

• (incorrect) That firm has **over** 3,000 employees.

• (correct) That firm has **more than** 3,000 employees.

OXYMORON

This fancy word means a phrase (usually two words) in which one word contradicts the meaning of the other. From Greek *oxus* (sharp) and *moros* (foolish, dull). Examples: deserted home, deafening silence, almost exact, pretty ugly, honest politician, greater (or larger) half, vacuum packed, live recording, automobile outdoor showroom, etc. Say: *OX-ee-MORE-on.*

PAIR/PAIRS

The word is singular; in referring to more than one, an *s* is required.

• (incorrect) He received two **pair** of socks.

• (correct) He received two **pairs** of socks.

PARAMETER/PERIMETER

The former is a word now — or recently — in style in the world of high-tech or businessese. A respected, recently published dictionary defines it this way: a variable or an arbitrary constant appearing in a mathematical expression, each value of which restricts or determines the specific form of the expression.

That ought to finish you off for good, as far as using this word. It should make you think about whether you don't really mean **perimeter** (from *peri*, meaning around, and *meter*, meaning measure). A **perimeter** is the line around the outside of an area and also the length of such a line, hence the boundaries or limits of an area or — by extension — of a problem or proposal.

PAST PARTICIPLE

This is dangerous territory. You may or may not precisely remember from your school days this name for a part of speech, specifically, that form of the verb which is used after *have* (or *be*) and which deals with action in the past.

The problem: Using the *past tense* of an irregular verb *in place of* the **past participle**.

A warning signal is sent to the listener when some form of the verb *have* is spoken, for immediately following that, your true colors are showing. So caution (and practice) is needed.

Forms of *have* are: *have, had, shall have, would have, will have* and *had had*. They all function in the same way as *have*.

You must be at ease with these past participles. (For contrast, the simple past tense form of the verb is also given, second column.)

Suggested practice (better, aloud): I **arose** early yesterday; I *have* **arisen** at 6:30 for years. And, continue all the way through the list.

Verb	Past	Past Participle
arise	arose	arisen
awake	There are several choices and lots of confusion; we suggest that you use **wake** (see).	
bear (to carry)	bore	born
beat	beat	beaten
become	became	become
begin	began	begun
bid	bid	bidden
bite	bit	bitten
blow	blew	blown
break	broke	broken
bring	brought	brought
burst	burst	burst
choose	chose	chosen
cling	clung	clung
come	came	come
creep	crept	crept
dive	dived (or dove)	dived
do	did	done
drag	dragged	dragged
draw	drew	drawn
dream	dreamed	dreamt
drink	drank	drunk
drive	drove	driven
dwell	dwelled	dwelled
eat	ate	eaten
fall	fell	fallen
fling	flung	flung

Verb	Past	Past Participle
fly	flew	flown
forbid	forbade or forbad	forbidden
forget	forgot	forgotten
forsake	forsook	forsaken
freeze	froze	frozen
get	got	gotten
give	gave	given
go	went	gone
grow	grew	grown
hang (trans.)	hung	hung
hang (intrans.)	hung	hung
hang (execute)	hanged	hanged
know	knew	known
lay	laid	laid
lean	leaned	leaned
leap	leaped (or leapt*)	leaped (or leapt*)
lend	lent	lent
lie (recline)	lay	lain
lie (tell falsehood)	lied	lied
light	lit	lit
plead	pleaded or pled	pleaded or pled
prove	proved	proven/proved**
rid	rid	rid
ride	rode	ridden
ring	rang	rung

* may be pronounced either *leapt* or *lept*.

proved is preferred; as an adjective (a **proven theory), *proven* is the word.

Verb	Past	Past Participle
rise	rose	risen
run	ran	run
saw	sawed	sawn
see	saw	seen
set	set	set
shake	shook	shaken
shine (trans.)	shined	shined*
shine (intrans.)	shone	shone**
show	showed	shown***
shrink	shrank	shrunk
sing	sing	sung
sink	sank	sunk
sit	sat	sat
slay	slew	slain
slide	slid	slid
sneak	sneaked	sneaked
speak	spoke	spoken
speed (verb)	sped	sped
steal	stole	stolen
sting	stung	stung
stink	stank or stunk	stunk
stride	strode	stridden

*Transitive verbs require a direct object.

- I *shined* the brass for the party.

**Intransitive verbs do not require a direct object.

- The sun *shone* yesterday.

*** *showed* is also approved by some authors, but *shown* sounds far better.

Verb	Past	Past Participle
strive	strove	striven
swear	swore	sworn
swell	swelled	swollen
swim	swam	swum
swing	swung	swung
take	took	taken
tear	tore	torn
throw	threw	thrown
wake (trans.)	wake	waked
wake (intrans.)	woke	waked
wear	wore	worn
weave	wove	woven
wring	wrung	wrung
write	wrote	written

PATIO

In the U.S. southwest, the word is widely accepted without a bad reaction — you almost never hear anything else, even from educated and cultured people. But in the rest of the country, it is just plain not very classy. Use *terrace* or even *veranda*.

It you can't break the habit, be sure to give **patio** a *t* sound *not* a *d*.

PEOPLE/PERSONS

In some uses, the words are interchangeable. But, generally, you will sound better if you use **people** for a group of individuals referred to as a group in an indefinite way.

- The struggling **people** of northern Africa...

Use **persons** where a specific and usually small number is called for.

PER

Two meanings, the first commonly acceptable in ordinary speech. The first is: to, for or by each ($3.00 **per** pound). The second is: according to (**per** your instructions); this use is better confined to business *correspondence.* In speaking, it sounds far better to use: according to, in accordance with, or (simpler) as instructed or requested.

PERSONALIZED

One of the all-too-many fancy and almost needlessly coined words to be avoided whenever possible. Ask yourself: can I use *personal*? Or, if the meaning is to mark with a person's initials, try *initialed* or *monogrammed.* If marked with his name, try *personal.*

The **-ize** (see) words are typical supposedly "high-tech" talk to create the air of big business. In actuality, they are a give-away, revealing the speaker as one who is trying to impress. He does impress, but in most cases, negatively.

See also **FINALIZE**.

PLURAL (WORDS IN A SERIES)

We have no trouble saying, "Bob, Joe and I are going home." But watch out for numbers, for, somehow, there's a tendency to slip incorrectly into the singular.

- (incorrect) Eleven, eight, six and three *is* 28.

- (correct) Eleven, eight, six and three *are* 28.

PLUS

If you want to sound like a second-rate radio commer-cial, use **plus** to mean *and* or *in addition to*. **Plus** should be reserved for mathematics. Yet you hear it all too often in TV or radio commercials or see it in printed ads, "**plus** you get a gift with every $100 purchase." Cheap, common and "commercial" sounding. Beyond that, do not begin a sentence with **plus**.

Incidentally, in arithmetic, the preposition **plus**, does *not* make the subject plural; seven (the unit of counting or measurement) **plus** three, *makes*, not *make*, ten.

PODIUM/LECTERN

It comes from the Greek *pod* meaning foot (a *podiatrist* is one who treats feet), and Latin *ped* in *pedestal, pedal, pedestrian.* Today it means foot, base, stage or platform. The speakers at a big meeting sit on, or step up onto, a **podium** to speak.

The tall desk, often with a light and a microphone, which speakers use to hold their papers (and to lean on) is a **lectern**.

So the airline employee who pages someone to "please come to the **podium**," almost always means **lectern**, *desk or counter.*

POINT/ TIME/PERIOD

The word **point** has two general meanings, one related to space and one related to time. The first is the invisible dot where two lines cross; hence we say, "The distance from this **point** to that **point** is x."

In the other context, the meaning is synonymous with instant, moment or time:

- At that **point**, the loudspeaker system went dead.

- At this **point**, gentlemen, our negotiations are at a standstill.

Or equally correct: At this **time**, gentlemen ...

But there is no need ever to use **point in time**; it's as silly as saying "see you next Tuesday of the week."

Although this is not totally logical, please believe that **point in time** is wince material and is to be avoided — even though the phrase has been a favorite of the federal government since the '60's. **Period** means *a space of time.* Hence, no *of time* is ever used.

- (incorrect) During that **period of time**, the sales increased.

- (correct) During that **period**, the sales increased.

PORTENTOUS/PRETENTIOUS

Portentous has to do with something significant, often calamitous, about to happen. Also, foreboding or causing awe. Not to be confused with **pretentious,** meaning putting on airs, self-important, claiming distinction usually unwarranted; showy.

PRACTICALLY

It means effectively or in a practical manner or in actual practice. It is too often used when *nearly* or *almost* is what is meant.

- We were **practically** (say *nearly*, *almost*) at the motel when the car broke down.

PREDOMINATE/PREDOMINANT

The verb means to be above, to have greater power. Don't confuse it with an adjective **predominant**, meaning outstanding, most noticeable, most important.

PREMIERE

See **FOREIGN WORDS**.

PREREQUISITE/PERQUISITE

Something required in advance.

- Math 101 is a **prerequisite** of (or for) Math 201.

Don't confuse it with **perquisite** which means a benefit that goes with rank or office, such as a car or parking space.

- In former days, the executive washroom was a **perquisite** for upper management.

PRESCRIBE/PROSCRIBE

Here's a device to help. Think of the first word in connection with those physician's orders (written in Sanskrit) which you take to the pharmacy. The doc is, in effect, *ordering* you to take certain medicines, i.e. a prescription.

So **prescribe** means to order or to set forth as a rule to be followed, as to things to be done.

Note that we're not talking about what is prohibited or condemned. That's what **proscribed** means. World of difference.

A speaker or writer can unwittingly be the deserved butt of a joke if he's not careful as to how he chooses and how he sounds.

PRESTIGE/PRESTIGIOUS

The former (a noun) means prominence or a status of influence. Since it is a noun, it is ordinarily not used to modify another noun, especially if a worthy adjective already exits — and it does. **Prestigious**, an adjective, means *having* **prestige**.

- (incorrect) A **prestige** apartment...

- (correct) A **prestigious** apartment...

See **FASHION/FASHIONABLE**.

PRETTY

Overly, overly used in the sense of *somewhat*. See also **GET/GOT**.

PREVENTIVE

Preventive (adjective) measures are actions made to help prevent some undesirable occurrence. There is no need to use the fancy-sounding *preventative*.

PROHIBIT/FORBID

Prohibit should always be followed by a noun (*not* by to or by *from*).

- (incorrect) Joe was **prohibited** *from* making additional loans.

- (correct) Bank rules **prohibit** loans to that firm.

- (correct) He will **prohibit** *hunting* on his land.

Forbid applies to *people*, and is followed by *to* or by the gerund (verb form), not by *from.*

- (correct) I **forbid** *you* to speak.

- (correct) I **forbid** your *speaking.*

- (incorrect) I **forbid** *you* from speaking.

PRONE/SUPINE

The former means either (a) likely to, or (b) lying (not laying) flat, face *down* (**prostrate**).

- He is **prone** to become flustered under pressure.

- He is **prone** on the floor.

Lying face *up* is **supine**.

PROSTRATE/PROSTATE

How to sound illiterate in one easy lesson! The former, an adjective, means lying flat, face down (**prone**).

Prostate, a noun, means a small troublesome gland surrounding the urethra at the base of the male bladder.

So undergoing a **prostrate** operation means that the surgery was performed while you were lying (not laying) face down. Careful — bet you meant a **prostate** operation.

PROVED/PROVEN

(See also **PAST PARTICIPLE**) I have **proved**, your honor, that the testimony is true. Correct. What about our friend **proven**? Reserve it for (a) a **proven** theory, now beyond question, and (b) a **proven** oil field (yep, there's oil there).

PROVIDED/PROVIDING

Both are correct but **provided** sounds better.

- The students may leave the campus **provided** that all term papers are handed in.

PROXIMITY

This means nearness of one thing or another. It is silly, then, to say *near* or *close* **proximity**; nobody would say "near nearness," would *he* (not *they*)?

QUALITY

This is a noun. It has two meanings.

(1) A particular characteristic, attribute or feature of someone or something.

- His warm voice is the **quality** of that politician which makes people like and trust him.

(2) Excellence, superiority, of very top grade. This is a somewhat rare use.

- The Duchess is a lady of true **quality**.

The problem comes from taking a short-cut and leaving out words.

"Mr. Buyer, we make only a **quality** product." But one may ask, "Of what **quality**?" Shoddy **quality**? Over-engineered **quality**? Unreasonably expensive **quality**? And we have a noun modifying a noun.

So **quality** by misuse has become common, trite and cheapened to the point where a phrase such as "we sell a **quality** storm window" means nothing. Does "**quality** education" mean that we should educate **quality**?

The best advice is to use it very sparingly, and when it is used, be sure that you don't make it modify another noun. Furthermore, define what **quality** you're trying to emphasize (reliable, luxurious, rugged, poor, superior, etc.).

QUESTION (noun)/ASK

In almost every use, this word can be omitted after **ask**, which means to inquire or inquire about.

- (correct) He **asked** the Senator (not: a **question**) about taxes.

QUICK/SLOW

Quick as an adverb (Run **quick**!) is correct, but *quickly* (and *slowly*) sound ever so much better.

RAISED/REARED

In discussing children, the two verbs are being blurred by common use. But cattle are **raised** and you'll sound better if you have **reared** kids.

RARELY/RARELY EVER

It means infrequently, seldom, not often. The phrase **rarely ever** doesn't make sense and sounds bad. Instead of "Joe **rarely ever** drinks," just say "Joe **rarely** drinks."

RAVEL

To unweave, to undo, to separate the threads of a cloth. Also, to fray. So *unravel* becomes redundant and unnecessary.

REAL/REALLY

The word **real** means true, valid, actual, not artificial. It is an adjective, a form of speech used primarily to modify a noun.

- The **real** diamond, meanwhile, was safely locked in a vault.

Adjectives in a series, must be separated by commas.

- The **real**, unvarnished, unpleasant facts of the crime are...

What is heard too often is the incorrect use of **real** (as an adverb) to mean *very*.

- (incorrect) He's a **real** fat man.

- (correct) He's a **really** fat man.

But **really** is overused to the point of having a trite sound. How much better it is to use *unusually, surprisingly, extremely, very* or other words.

REASON (BECAUSE)

See **BECAUSE/REASON**.

REASON/SINCE/BECAUSE/AS

There are at least three ways to say *the reason that.* They are: **as**, **since** (see) and **because** (see). Consider:

- **As** it was snowing, I zipped up my wool jacket.

  Was the zipping done *during* the snowfall, or was it **because** of the snow? Our guess is **because**.

- **Since** I was walking on the long, hot road, I was very thirsty.

  Were you thirsty ever **since** the walk or **because** of it? Our guess is **because**.

Since is better left to deal only with the duration of time, a moment in the past to the present.

REDUNDANCY

Saying the same thing twice. Here's a common error: I have a friend of mine who... The fact that you *have* a friend makes the friend yours; the *of mine* just repeats what you have already said or written. Take your pick, but don't use both, because this widely heard error sounds very wrong.

Other examples include such boo-boos as advance forward, advance planning, alternate back and forth, and et cetera, anticipate in advance, ask a question, assemble together, beside one another, blow of wind, brief summary (or summation), brief synopsis, brief vignette (*say: veen-yet*), calories (or BTUs) of heat, cancel (each other) out, cantilevered out, chowder soup, close (or near) proximity, cluster together, co-author (or co-sponsor) jointly.

Also: communicate back and forth, complete and comprehensive, complete stop, connect together, consensus of opinion, consolidate together, continue on, convicted felon, coordinate together, core essentials, cross over, currently (busy) at this time, delete out, deport out, descend down, dialog with, difficult obstacles, divert aside (or away), drowned (or suffocated) to death, elevate up, end result, enter into.

And: entire gamut, epilogue at the end, escalate up, exact replica, exact same, exit out, false lies, false myth, fiery inferno, filled to capacity, final destination, final outcome, finally finish, foreign import (or export), foresee in advance, forever and ever, forward progress (or planning), free gift, from whence (whence means "from where"), frozen solid, future planning (i.e., *about* the future), future prediction (or prognosis), gather together, geisha girl, globally around the world, grocery store, handwritten manuscript, hot water heater, illegal bootlegging (or counterfeiting).

Also: import in, include in, incremental growth, indoor showroom, initiated (or created) for the first time, interpersonal relationship, intersection of two (or more) roads, Jewish rabbi, join together, juxtaposition together (or side by side in juxtaposition), kill (someone) dead, knots per hour, lag behind, last and final, lead ahead, lift up, link together, log (or board) of wood, longer in length, lower (verb) down, meal of food, mental telepathy, merge together, moment in time (or five years time), mutual agreement, neighboring (or suburban or surrounding) environs or suburbs, net (or final) result, never in (my) life, new and novel, newborn neonatal, new discovery, new initiative.

And: new innovation, new record, old adage, old cliche, old maxim, one and the same, one (or each) individual, opening gambit, original creation, originally (or previously or already) established, oven baked, overexaggerate, paid staff, pan fried, paperback book, past history, past (or previous) precedent, personal belongings, personal friend, personal opinion, personal resignation, personally, I feel (or believe), pizza pie, please RSVP, point in (or period of) time, pre-dinner cocktail, pre-plan (or pre-plan in advance), prior experience, project forward (or out), propped up, prudent and wise, raining outside, rally back, rather instead, rebate back, recessed back, recur again (or over and over), refer back, reflect (or recollect or remember) back, religious holiday.

Also: repay back, repeat (or reiterate) again, replace back, replica copy, reply back, required prerequisite, respond back, restore back, return back, revert back, rice paddy, Rio (river) Grande River, rise up, safe haven, safety and security, same identical, school student, second runner-up, security protection, separate out, sherry (or port) wine, shrimp scampi, sink down, sit (or fall) down, slide down, smile on (the, his) face, soaking wet, step in and intervene, stoop down, subtle innuendo, sugar diabetes, sum total, surrounded on all sides, team together, temporary pause, termination point (meaning time), the year 1994 (etc.), time period, timeless and enduring, today's soup du jour, ton of weight, trail behind, trained experts, transient coming and going.

And: true facts, trusted confidant, tuna fish, twins who are both 18, two-way dialogue, unexpected surprise, unified (or unite) together, unwanted trespassers, urban cities, visibly (or visually) see, volt (or watt) of energy (or electricity), wider in width, yellow jaundice, young whelp, your own personal (anything), etc.

One we particularly like is "intermittent showers on and off throughout the day."

REFERENCE

The meaning of this noun is well understood by every-one, but it is included here as an example of business people who use "Verbspeak" (the incorrect use of nouns as verbs). Thus, we learn that the memo *refer-enced* the earlier contract. The correct phrase, obvi-ously, is *referred to* or *made reference to*, but the wrong use is an insult to the ear. See also the lan-guage called **BUSINESSESE**.

REGARD(S)

There is such a word as **regards**; it means greetings or best wishes, as in the song *Give My Regards to Broad-way*. But when *about* or *in reference to* is meant, the word is **regard**, no *s* ever.

• In **regard** to the expense involved…

But, *as* **regards** *to* is correct.

RETICENT/RELUCTANT

Reticent people don't *like* to speak up; **reluctant** people are generally *unwilling* to do something.

RISE/RAISE

Best advice is to use the **rise** only in the intransitive sense, i.e., something **rises** in height or value. But you don't **rise** anything.

Raise (verb) should be confined to the transitive sense, i.e., you **raise** something. As a noun, it is confined to that welcome increase in salary

- (incorrect) When it rains, the water in the river will **raise** up.

- (correct) When it rains, the water in the river will **rise**.

RSVP

Although an acronym for French (*repondez, s'il vous plait*), this has become rather common English. It means "Reply (answer), if you please," or, more simply, "Please reply."

So saying or writing "Please **RSVP**" means "Please please reply," which is redundant and wrong.

SAME/IDENTICAL

Either word is fine for describing the relationship between two things, but not both; a pure redundancy.

- (incorrect) He bought the **same identical** thing.

- (correct) He bought the **same** thing.

- (correct) He bought the **identical** thing.

SEMI

A combining form (example, semiannual) meaning half, partial or twice in a named period.

Thus semiannual is equivalent to biannual (happening twice a year).

Say: *SEM-ee*

SERIES (LIST)

"The thief stole records, tapes, recorders and broke the rear window." Problem: the sentence lists *records, tapes, recorders* and *broke* as all being equivalent, parallel to each other; obviously they are not. So we have an illogical and wrong construction. Solution: insert *and* just before *recorders*.

SERVICE/SERVE

As a verb, **service** has two meanings. The most commonly used one is to repair or attend to something, so as to help assure its continuing operation. When the washing machine quits, you probably call for someone to **service** it. You might also call the **service** man once a year, or so, to lubricate it, inspect it for wear, etc. We're all glad that elevators are **serviced** on a regular schedule.

Those few who have farm backgrounds will remember that a dairy farmer would take one of his cows somewhere from time to time, to be **serviced** by a neighboring bull.

This latter point is made here to emphasize that using **service** when you mean **serve** can cause considerable confusion and occasionally a laugh (Agony Airlines now **services** Louisville).

Louisville isn't broken in the first place, and we'll skip the barnyard interpretation!

Waiters, flight attendants, sales clerks in stores, and the like, **serve** you — or are supposed to. What they and their employers provide is the noun, **service**.

The verb distinction is an important one.

SET/SIT

People do *not* **set** down to eat; they **sit**. The exceptions are: the sun **sets**, concrete **sets** and hens **set** on eggs. **Set** also means to put or place. And it sounds better to have a *thing* **set** (remain) on top of something else, rather than **sit**.

SHOWCASE

It's a noun and it means the obvious: a display case or box, usually glass, to exhibit articles. It's the *verb* use that jars the ear. There's no need to **showcase** the new products or whatever, when we can display, show, exhibit, demonstrate, feature, set forth, introduce, etc., them.

See also **NOUNSPEAK**.

SIMPLE/SIMPLISTIC

We all understand that **simple** means uncomplicated, easy, unadorned, not combined. But sometimes there is a temptation to try to impress listeners with long words (method-methodology, use-utilize, etc.). It's not a good idea because the speaker usually sounds pretentious and uneducated, exactly the opposite of the desired impression.

Simplistic means that something is *oversimplified* by someone ignoring the real complexities or possible implications.

Remember that *-istic* endings mean *as if*, or *pretending* to be something. A *realistic* setting in the theater is one that *seems* to be real, but of course we know it isn't. So a **simplistic** solution *only pretends* to be simple.

The words aren't synonyms, so choose carefully.

SINCE

It means, most commonly, *from then until now*. How does this sound: **Since** the opening of the larger California factory, Bill *took* a more aggressive market plan. Wrong. It should be *has taken*.

SLOW

See **QUICK/SLOW**.

SOMEONE ELSE'S

- (incorrect) By error, he took **someone's else** hat.

- (correct) By error, he took **someone else's** hat.

This is without grammatical logic, but common usage has made it *as* (not *like*) it is.

SORT

See **TYPE /STYLE/SORT/KIND OF**.

SUBJUNCTIVE

Chances are good that you've forgotten the subjunctive mood for verbs, as explained by Miss Winterwhistle back in the fifth grade. It's the verb form that deals with situations that (a) state a wish, possibility or supposition *contrary to fact*, and (b) deal with requests or commands.

- (incorrect) If I *was* President...

- (correct) If I *were* President... (the fact is that you are not).

This is important because the *was* rings out loud and clear, and labels the speaker as ignorant. For the second use, remember the old — but proper — way to end a meeting.

- (incorrect) I move that the meeting *is* adjourned.

- (correct) I move that the meeting *be* adjourned.

Other examples (correct):

- She asked that he *give* in on this point.

- The divorcee filed a suit asking that the former husband *pay* for child support.

If I *were* you, I'd study this point.

Here's another boo-boo that is frequently heard.

"If Joe would have (or "of") been there earlier..." But Joe was *not* there earlier; hence, a statement contrary to fact, therefore, subjunctive called for.

- (correct) If Joe **had** been there earlier...

SURE

Consider the choice:

- Be **sure** *and* call when you arrive.

- Be **sure** *to* call when you arrive.

The phrase **be sure** should be followed by the infinitive (*to* call). And, beyond that, it sounds better.

SURE/SURELY

It's an adjective (he's a **sure** winner) so the use of **sure** to modify a verb (he's **sure** going to win) is wrong and sounds so. **Surely** is the adverb needed.

TAKE/BRING

Use the first one to mean carry *away*, and the latter to mean carry *back* this way (toward the speaker).

TERRIBLY/AWFULLY

Originally, causing terror or awe. They are now diluted to mean *extreme* to the point that an ordinary cup of coffee is **terribly** — or **awfully** — good. Note how very often the words are used, and, therefore, how stale they have become. That applies to any very over-worked word, and calls for some effort to break the habit, and find substitute words that have significant meaning. Same idea applies to the over-used *terrific*.

THAN

Caution is needed in choosing the pronoun to follow **than**, since it can be used as either a preposition or a conjunction. The problem, and the misuse, comes when the sentence contains implied (rather than stated) elements. Here you must determine the meaning of the sentence in order to choose the proper pronoun. The following sentences are both correct, but they have different meanings.

- She likes him more **than** I.

- She like him more **than** me.

The first sentence carries the meaning that she likes him more *than I do,* so *I* is the subject of an *imagined verb.* In the second example, **than** is a preposition and she doesn't like *me* as much as she likes *him.*

THAT (ALL)

Leaving this out of a dependent clause results in your saying very confusing sentences.

- (incorrect) What's really important is if the men feel strongly about the seniority rule, they'll strike.

- (correct) What's really important is **that** if the men feel strongly about the seniority rule, they'll strike.

Another set of examples

- (incorrect) In the new contract, the important difference is it provides better salaries.

- (correct) In the new contract, the important difference is **that** it provides better salaries.

Another ear-grating error occurs when **that** and *it* both appear. Omit the *it.*

- (incorrect) It's the type of injury **that**, if he continues to play, *it* could lead to paralysis.

Avoid the totally ambiguous **all that** in: The movie we saw wasn't **all that** good; omit **all**.

THEIR/HIS/HER

You hear this mistake often.

- (incorrect) Did anyone forget **their** hat?

- (correct) Did anyone forget **his** hat?

This is assuming only one hat was found; if two or more were left behind, put an *s* on hat and leave the **their** as is, i.e., *several* heads and, therefore, *several* hats.

- Did any of the guests forget **their** hats?

But *anyone* has only one head and only one hat. It's singular. Therefore use **his** if it's a male or mixed group and **her** if it's a female group.

THEMSELF/THEIRSELF

Several readers of this little guide may, understandably, be insulted by the inclusion of this and similar obvious items. We apologize; there is no way to know which of our readers would be prone to make such errors.

Our consolation is that we believe that no reader will avoid *every* error that we set forth herein.

Theirself, *theirselves* and *hisself* do not exist.

- (incorrect) At the buffet, the guests served **theirselves**.

- (correct) At the buffet, the guests served **themselves** (not **themself**).

- (correct) At the buffet, each guest served **himself** (not **themselves**).

Remember: We (plural) helped *ourselves* (plural) not *ourself* (singular).

THERE IS/ARE

This mistake is often made, usually by an uneducated small-town boy who has made it to professional baseball or football. And that is what you *don't* want to sound like!

- (incorrect) **There's** at least three guys on the team who feel that way.

- (correct) **There are** at least three guys on the team who feel that way.

Remember: **There is one**... and **there are** *two or more*. The trap is even easier to fall into using the more familiar, conversational contractions *there's* and *they're*.

The same common sense applies to the past tense of *is*:

- (incorrect) **There** *was* two reporters waiting for him at the plane.

- (correct) **There** *were* two reporters waiting for him at the plane.

So when you hear, "serving on that committee, **there is** Joe, Harry and Betty," you are hearing a common error.

Keep in mind, too, that the words like *several, many, a lot*, etc., are obviously plural.

- (incorrect) **There is** (or **there's**) several left in the carton.

- (correct) **There are** several left in the carton

THIS

Keep in mind that, upon hearing the word **this**, the listener's mind and attention are drawn to something *near* or *close* in time. So after a sentence like: At the library, she saw **this** book on hypnosis... almost all listeners will look at the speaker to see him holding the book. But he does not have the book in hand and never intended to.

Another common error in less educated speech: He

met **this** cute girl... But the girl is not at hand or even nearby.

What is meant, in the preceding two examples, is *a* book and *a* cute girl.

This **this** is one of those wrong-sounding giveaways.

Also, be aware of the confusing and odd-sounding effect when **this** is omitted altogether..

- (incorrect): The whole thing is can we make the project pay off?

- (better) The whole thing is **this:** can we make the project pay off?

The use of **this** avoids phrases like: "the idea is make the public aware." The "is make" problem can also be avoided by "idea (or plan) is to make."

See also **THAT(ALL)**.

TILL/UNTIL

In writing if you use **till**, remember two *l's*. Easy gimmick: if you add *un*, you're "entitled" to drop one *l*.

TO BE + PRONOUN

This verb causes some trouble because of the pronoun that follows. Technically, "it was I" is correct. If that scares you, do please have the courage to use *I* when the sentence is expanded. These are correct:

- It was (or *is*) **I** who sent him the first letter.

- It was **they** who opened the negotiations.

- It was **he** who predicted the outcome.

- It was **she** who was doubtful from the beginning.

You may feel shaky on the *I/me* standing alone, but don't waver a bit on the others. It was *them, her, him, us* all sound illiterate.

TOGETHER WITH/AND

(Also *as well as, in addition to, including, with* and *plus.*)

These words do *not* make a singular subject become plural. They are, in effect, a kind of whispered "aside" to the reader, a statement in parentheses.

- NBC, **together with** its affiliates, *is* taking a stand on showing the film.

But **and** does *not* fall into this category.

- NBC **and** CBS *are* going to show the film.

TOWARD/TOWARDS

Both are correct; the former sounds better, a little more refined.

TRANSLUCENT

It passes light (the opposite of opaque), but does not mean transparent (clear, like pure glass).

TRANSMUTE

You see in the word the stem *mute*, as in *mutate* (to change) and *mutation* (the process of being altered, or the change itself). Don't confuse **transmute** with *transmit* (to send along unchanged).

TRANSPIRE

"Hey, Joe, what **transpired** at the meeting?" We hear this often, but the truth is that the word means to come to be known, or come to light. The events at the meeting happened, occurred or came to pass.

TRY AND/TO

Try to finish before 5:00 sounds much, much better than **try and**. A fine point but worth remembering.

TYPE/STYLE/SORT/KIND OF

You would never say "this sort book..." or "this kind candy..." and you're right. So, you should follow **type** and **style** with **of** rather than trying to turn them into failed adjectives. Also, never add *a* after the **of**.

- (incorrect) That **type** house...

- (incorrect) That **type of** a house...

- (correct) That **type of** house...

Refined conversation uses **kind** in place of **type** (that **kind** of book), and avoids uses such as "a new, memory-type typewriter."

Beware the plural; it's never "*these/those* **type/style/ sort/kind of** book (or books)" Make it *this/that* **type**, etc. See also **KIND OF**.

UNAWARE/UNAWARES

The former means not being aware of, unconscious of.

- Joe was **unaware** that he was being watched.

With an *s* it means by surprise, suddenly, unexpectedly.

- The man leaped from behind the bushes and grabbed Joe **unawares**.

But never the twain should meet.

- (incorrect) Joe was **unawares** that I was in the room.

- (correct) Joe was **unaware** that I was in the room.

UNIQUE

One of a kind, there being no other like it. The *uni* is obviously Latin for *one* as in *uniform* and *unity*. Don't use it to mean odd, peculiar, unusual, etc. There are many adjectives to fill that need.

Therefore, the following do not make sense: *very* **unique**, *more* **unique**, *nearly* **unique.** It's either one of a kind or it isn't. This is a commonly heard error.

In the same vein, there are some other words which, under normal circumstances should not be qualified (by using, *more, nearly, less, almost, completely,* etc.): *perfect, final, fatal, exact, unanimous, round, absolute, eternal, complete, straight, perpendicular, unlimited.* In the cold light of day, we would all agree that *more fatal* (or *dead* or *pregnant*) makes no sense, but it's good to ponder some of the silly things people say without thinking.

UNNECESSARY WORDS

Habit leads nearly everyone into these kinds of un-needed clutter:

To **cut** is to sever or divide, usually by a knife, etc. Why add *up*?

To **finish** is to bring to an end, to complete, to terminate. Why add *up*?

To **beat** is to punch, thrash, etc. Why add *up*?

To **start** is to begin, to commence, to undertake. Why add *up* or *off*?

To **slow** is to reduce speed, to retard. Why add *down*? Or, even stranger, *up*?

To **speed** is to hasten, to move rapidly. Why add *up*?

To **find** is to come upon, to discover. Why add *out*?

More

Boost up, call up (meaning to telephone), chew up, clean up, close down, continue on, cool down, dry out, end up, figure out, fill up, find out, focus in, free up, freeze up, hang up, heat up, head up (a committee) , help out, high up, hurry up, include in, join up, loosen up, melt down, over with, pick out, queue up, rain-shower activity, reduce down, save up, seek out, sit down, stand up, start off/up/out, team up, want for you to, write down or to write up (your report).

UPWARD/UPWARDS

The sales chart showed an **upward** (never **upwards**) trend. **Upwards** means more than or exceeding or over. He paid **upwards** of (i.e., *over*) $200,000 for that house.

US/WE

Now and then (usually when trying to talk in a "folksy" way), a speaker will slide into an incorrect use of the objective **us** for the nominative **we**. If so, we hear the jarring, "**Us** farmers would rather have too much rain than too little." Obviously, "**We** farmers would..." is correct.

USE/USED

Consider: We (**use**) (**used**) to do business with them years ago. In that sentence, **use** has the meaning of *make a practice of*. Since the example refers to the past, think of *made a practice*, hence **used** (which is correct) not **use**.

UTILIZE

(Meaning **use**.) This unnecessarily long and fake tech-sounding word is heard all too often when good old *use* is perfect — and is all that is needed. Maybe it will take a best friend to tell you about your own habit; hearing oneself is difficult.

So much for 95%. The remaining one narrow, rather special occasion for **utilize**, lies in its meaning to turn into practical benefit something which formerly or normally *would not have been used*.

- The natives learned to **utilize** the stalk and husk (of the grain plant after harvest) for fertilizer and mulch.

VERBAL

The word literally means having to do with words; it *can* mean written *or* spoken. But if you want to be exact in speaking of some agreement that was talked over and not written, then it's best to use the specific term *oral*.

WAIT FOR/WAIT ON

This is one of these all-too-revealing differences that we call "give aways" in this book (i.e., they give you away as one who doesn't know).

In a restaurant or shop, someone **waits on** you. Later, having a date with a friend (who is late), you **wait for** him to arrive.

This will be obvious and unneeded to most of our readers, but the difference is absolutely vital.

WAKE

The verb is both transitive (we were told to **wake** Bill at seven) and intransitive (we **wake** [you can add *up*, but you don't need it] early in summer). The past tense is *woke, waked* or *wakened* — take your pick; there is a small preference for the verb forms with *en* when used in the passive voice (she was *wakened* early).

Wake may have the prefix a as in *awake, awaken, awoke,* etc. There is a small preference for the form with this *a* when the verb is used figuratively (i.e., not literally); he *awoke* to the danger too late. When the verb is used both passively and figuratively, the much preferred form is *awakened*. (Bill has been *awakened* to the threat.)

WANT FOR

Although somewhat more accepted in the backwoods, and even more so in the South, this plain mistake says "ungrammatical hill-billy" to the hearer.

- (incorrect) I **want for** you to…

- (correct) I **want** you to…

The same applies to *like for, would like for* and *need for.*

WAY/WAYS (A)

No one would argue against *a* meaning *one* (a book; two books). Yet, you will hear a surprising number of people say, "We have *a* long **ways** to go." There does not seem to be any explanation for the error, heard more often in rural areas.

WHAT

The most common misuse is the insertion of **what** when it is not needed (and wrong).

- (incorrect) The book was much bigger than **what** he had originally imagined.

- (correct) The book was much bigger than he had originally imagined.

WHEN/ WHERE/ IN WHICH

Be careful to choose the right one and none other.

- (time) It was at that critical *time* in his young life **when** he had to make a career choice.

- (place) It's that *fork* in the road near the bridge **where** you start to climb the long hill.

- (place — inside) He wrote a long, detailed *report* **in which** he explained exactly what happened.

WHENEVER/WHEN

Keep in mind that **whenever** implies a *repeated* act, as opposed to something that normally occurs once.

- (correct) The dog barks **whenever** the doorbell rings.

But don't use it for a one time occurrence.

- (incorrect) He drove upstate for the funeral, and **whenever** he returned he found that his house had been burglarized.

- (correct) He drove upstate for the funeral, and **when** he returned he found that his house had been burglarized.

WHERE (MEANING THAT)

I read **where** they've just passed a law… Ouch. You read **where** there's a good reading light, *that's* **where** you read. The correct word is **that** as in, I read **that** they've just passed a law…

Same applies to: I heard, I saw, they said, etc.

And, "The study hall is the place **that** (or **in which**) the students prepare their lessons." This sounds much better than **where**.

WHETHER

The *or not* that so often is used after **whether**, is almost always unnecessary. (**Whether** *or not* the patent has expired is not known.) Omit the *or not* unless the meaning changes when *if* is substituted for **whether**. When that occurs, the *or not* is needed. (I'm going home **whether** Bill comes with me *or not*.)

WHICH

It is easier than you think to get lost in a long **which** sentence. And your listener will have a feeling of uneasiness and uncertainty about (a) your getting lost, and (b) how — if at all — you're going to get out of the jungle.

- (incorrect) He was always asking complicated questions **which** you were supposed to reply quickly and without any preparation.

- (correct) He was always asking complicated questions **to which** you were supposed to reply quickly and without any preparation.

- (incorrect) Bob belongs to several clubs **which** guests are restricted in terms of who they are, hours, etc.

- (correct) Bob belongs to several clubs **in which** guests are restricted in terms of who they are, hours, etc.

Along with the "dangling" **which**, beware the "dangling" **who** or **whom**.

WHICH/WHO/THAT

We obviously wouldn't say, "this is the man **which** phoned yesterday." **Which**, as we all know, refers to things (this is the window **which** is broken), but be careful about using **who** for non-persons: "**That** is the club **which** (not **who**) took in new members." **That** can be used for either people or things; it sounds better, though, if **that** if used for things.

WHO/WHOM

To even a semi-trained ear, the use of these words is a certain turn-off. Think of **who** being comparable to *he* and **whom** comparable to *him*.

You would surely (incorrectly) never say, "Throw the ball to *he*"; rather, you would say "to *him*" (the object of the preposition *to*). Just so, hearing, "to **who** did you write?" is wrong and should make you wince.

The following are correct:

- To **whom** shall I send this notice?

- **Whom** should they invite?

- The employee, **who** objected to the rule, filed an appeal.

- I don't care **whom** you ask.

Putting *he/him* in place of **who/whom** often quickly clarifies the issue. **Whoever/whomever** (see) *follow* **who/whom** *exactly*.

WHOEVER/WHOMEVER

The check will be paid by (**whoever**) (**whomever**) arrived last at the table. The preposition *by* should be followed by **whom** — right? Wrong! The entire *clause* (**whoever**...table) is the object of *by* — not the **whoever**; the **whoever** is the subject of *arrives*. Fooled you! Better practice on this one a bit.

Another example or two, both correct.

- The quarterback will throw to **whoever** is open. (**whoever** is the subject of *is*).

- Fran will invite **whomever** she likes (**whomever** is the object of *likes*).

-WISE

As an add-on to otherwise respectable words, this ending is overworked business jargon and sounds awful. There are a few words (*likewise*) which are accepted and go by unnoticed. But do avoid the contorted sounds of "**saleswise**, they're up 10%" or "**managementwise**, they're weak." You mean that the management is weak.

A cartoon some years ago said it all. A father owl, addressing mother owl about youngster owl, perched nearby, asks, "How's he doing wise-wise?"

WITH

The word is often unnecessary at the end of a sentence and makes the sentence sound cluttered and semi-literate. (The trial will soon be over **with**.)

WOMAN

George Jean Nathan, late drama critic for the *New York Times* once said, "In the theater, a hero is one who believes that all women are ladies. A villain is one who believes that all ladies are women."

See **LADY**.

WORN/WORE

In the sense of much used, frayed, or **worn** out, **worn** is fine. At all costs, avoid the incorrect and jarring: After the climb up that hill, I'm all **wore** out.

WOULD (OF) (HAVE)

Because **of** sounds something like **have** (and is easier to say), and because the speaker doesn't know any better, you often hear this mistake.

- (incorrect) I **would of** made it on time, except...

- (correct) I **would have** made it on time except...

Using **of** in this manner is dead wrong.

WRONG/WRONGLY

This is one of those common errors in which the adjective is used when the sentence is explaining how something is done (which means an adverb is a must).

- (incorrect) He was treated **wrong**.

- (correct) He was treated **wrongly**.

Similarly, watch out for *correct/incorrectly, quick/quickly, prompt/promptly*, etc.

YA KNOW

This meaningless, stall-for-time, annoying phrase has crept into daily speech, mostly plaguing teenagers. But beware — it could make *your* speech sound awful, and it might have invaded without *your* (not *you*) realizing the danger.

YET

The word **yet** is derived from German *jezt* (pronounced *yetz*) meaning *now*. In some areas of the country, where some influence of German heritage remains, you hear **yet** being used when *still* is what is meant.

If Betty is about halfway through a typing job, the question to her is, "Are you **still** typing that?" not, "Are you typing that **yet**?" Nonsense, because it's known that she started a good while ago.

YOURSELF

Does this sound normal? "Good morning, how are you today?" Of course it does. Yet we hear, in answer, "I'm fine; how's **yourself**?"

Words ending in *self* or *selves* should be confined to only two very special instances: (a) the reflexive use, in which the pronoun is turned back on the subject, and (b) the emphatic use.

- You cut **yourself** badly.

- Don't kid me; you saw the accident **yourself**!

So the reply to the early morning greeting is, "Fine, thank you. How are *you*?"

See also **MYSELF**.

Part 2
Pronounciation

ACCESS (NOUN AND VERB)

Be sure to start out "ack" not "eck" (as in *excess*).

ACCESSORY

Something that goes along with, or is used with, something else. Be sure that the first syllable is *ack* (like *pack*), so it's *ack-SESS-or-ee* (**not** *uh-SESS-or-ee*).

ACCIDENTALLY

This common adverb means by accident, chance, luck, etc.

The trick is that is has *five* syllables *ac-ci-dent-al-ly* (the adjective *accidental* has the adverb ending *ly* stuck on the end). It is often mispronounced *ac-ci-dent-ly*.

ACROSS

There is no *t* sound at the end of this word.

ADDRESS

As a noun (indicating 723 Main Street, for instance), the word stresses the first syllable *AD-dress*.

If a major speech is meant, accent the second syllable, and the same for the verb.

- He **addressed** (*ad-DRESSED*) the meeting.

AEGIS

Rule or authority or, sometimes, protection or responsibility.

- A variety of prevention, sanitation, education, and research activities all fall under the **aegis** of the U.S. Public Health Service.

Say: *EE-jis.*

AGRICULTURE

The second syllable of this work is often said *rah* instead of the correct *ri* (the *i* like in *pit*).

It's *AG-ri-cul-ture.*

ALIENATE

To cause someone to become estranged, unfriendly or indifferent. The trick is (a) it has four syllables *AY-lee-an-ate*, and (b) the first syllable is *ay* (like *hay*) not *al* (like *pal*).

ALTERNATE

Noun, meaning a person taking the place of another. It's *ALL-tur-nit.*

ALUMNA

Latin; a female graduate or former student. Say: *A-LUM-nah*. The plural is alumnae: *a-LUM-nee*.

ALUMNUS

Latin; a male graduate or former student. Say: *a-LUM-nuss*. The plural is alumni: *a-LUM-nigh*.

AMATEUR

Oh, my, how common this error is, and what an effect it has on the hearer!

There is no *ch* (as in *child*) sound in the middle of this word. It's *AM-uh-tur*. The last syllable is a dead rhyme for stir not pure.

AMENABLE

Agreeable; capable of being led or advised. The second syllable can be either *meen* or *men,* but the former of these is preferred. Say: *ah-MEEN-uh-bul*.

AMPHITHEATER

A small circular room to watch performances. The trick here is the often overlooked "ph" (pronounced "f" as in physical). *AM-fuh-THEE-uh-tur* (not *the often heard AMP-uh-THEE-uh-tur*).

ARCTIC

It is not *AR-tick* but *ARK-tic*.

ARTHRITIS

Remember three (not four) syllables. Say: *arth-RITE-iss.*

ASTERISK

The funny, bug-like mark used to indicate that the reader should look somewhere for a footnote. The problem is not so much the search for the footnote, but for pronouncing the word: it is not *AS-ter-ick* nor is it *AS-ter-ich.* The last syllable is *isk.* (Think of risk, which isn't a bad gimmick to remember... and to sound right.)

ATHLETE

Remember two (*not* three) syllables: *ATH-leet.* Also: *ath-LET-icks.*

AUTOMOBILE

The last syllable is pronounced *beel* not *bill.*

BANAL

Predictable; worn-out from repeated use; trite. Originally French. There are several pronunciations, but the preferred is: *buh-NAHL.*

BANTER

(Noun and verb) Light-hearted conversation, often involving good-natured teasing or kidding. Not to be confused with *bander,* a non-word.

BASIS

A foundation or chief component of anything — a fundamental ingredient or principle. *BAY-sis.* The plural (bases) is pronounced *BAY-seez.*

BEAUTIFUL/BEAUTY

Be careful to avoid a *d* sound and also an *ee* sound (*BYU-dee-ful*); it's a *t* sound at the start of the *tiff* syllable. Say: *BYU-tiff-ul* and *BYU-tee.*

BEIGE

The light tan color. It's *BAYZH*, with the *zh* sliding off like the end of *garage.* Avoid a "d" sound (*baydge,* like *bridge*). See **GE=ZH** in **FOREIGN WORDS**.

BERET

Originally French, now usual English. The round, wool cap (without visor). The first syllable is not *burr* but *bare*; the *et* (like *Chevrolet*) is *ay.*

BLASE

Bored or uninterested because the subject seems to be "old stuff." It has retained its original pronunciation: *blah-ZAY.*

BOULEVARD

Originally French, now long established English. The first syllable to be much preferred is *boo*, not *bull.* It's *BOO-luh-vahrd.*

BUFFET

See **FOREIGN WORDS**.

CATCH

Whether you are discussing a splendid baseball/ football play, a day's allotment of brook trout, or a miserable head cold, the word is always:

CAT-ch; never *KET* (like *pet* or *let*)-*ch*.

CATER-CORNERED

This is the correct word (not cata or kitty).

CAYENNE

This is the orange/red powder used to season foods; sometimes called "red pepper." It probably came originally from Cayenne, the capital of French Guiana in South America. You do hear *kay-en,* but *ky-en* gets the nod in preference.

CEMENT

The adhesive powder used to make concrete (which is what sidewalks, roads, etc., are made of). Also a verb, to bind or affix one thing to another.

The first syllable is not *see* and the accent is on the *last* syllable. It's *suh-MENT*.

CHASSIS

Originally French, now standard English. Most common use is the steel frame under a car to which the wheels and motor are attached, and on which the body rests.

It has kept enough of its French Connection so that the far better sound of the *ch* is *sh* (like *Chevrolet*, the French auto pioneer): *SHASS-ee*.

COMFORTABLE

Avoid the too-often heard *comf-tur-bull*. It's *COME-fort-a-bull*.

COMPANY

Three syllables, not two. It's *KUMP-uh-nee*. Same tip applies to "accompany."

COMPTROLLER

An officer of an organization who monitors financial matters. Also spelled *controller*. Both spellings are pronounced the same: *kon-TROL-er*.

CONGRATULATE

This does not have a *t, d,* or *j* (like *dredge*) sound. It's *konn-GRACH-u-late*.

CONNOISSEUR

A person with educated and discriminating taste, especially in arts, food, decor, etc. Beware the last syllable; it is not *sewer* but *sur* (like *fur*).

CORSAGE

Very small bouquet for the ladies to wear, usually pinned near the shoulder. The last syllable is *ahj*; the *j* slides off like the *z* in azure, the *s* in pleasure, or the end of garage. See **GE=ZH** in **FOREIGN WORDS**.

COSTUME

The first syllable is *kos,* not *kosh.*

COUPON

A little paper ticket, usually detached from something else, and of some value. Originally French, hence it keeps its connection on the first syllable, i.e. *KOO* (not *CUE) -pon.*

CREEK

A stream; remember the old memory trick: crick is hick. The stream rhymes with peek, seek, speak.

DAIS

A raised platform or podium, as in a meeting hall, usually with chairs so people are on view.

Say: *DAY-iss.*

See also **PODIUM/LECTURN** in **USAGE SECTION**.

DEBUT

As a noun, it is easily recognized as a first appearance, a beginning. As a verb, to begin or introduce some-thing. Say: *day-byue.*

DEBUTANTE

The young lady who has just made her debut. Say: *DAY-byew-tahnt.*

DEFECT

As a noun, it's a flaw or something imperfect. Say: *DEE-fect.* As a verb, it means to go over to the other (or opposing) side or nation. Say: *dee-FECT.*

DEFENSE

Protection against whatever; *dee-FENSE.*

DELUXE

Very elegant, top quality. It brings to mind the first syllable of *tuxedo* (or *tux* for short). But the final *e* does the same job it would do in English (pal vs. pale); it makes the *u* say *yew* (universe). So it's *duh-LOOKS*, avoiding, *dee-lux* (like *ducks*).

DEMUR/DEMURE

Demur, a verb, is pronounced *duh-MURR* (like *fur*). It means to take exception to, raise an objection to or object.

- All the other company directors were in favor of the motion, but George felt he had to **demur**.

Gimmick: Everybody's for the plan; you're not, so you **demur**; you're not *"fur"* it.

Sorry, but it may help.

Demure, an adjective, is pronounced *duh-MURE* (like *pure*). It means reserved, or pretending shyness and modesty.

- The shy young girl looked very **demure** in her pink dress.

The two words have *no* connection whatsoever.

DESCENT

It is not *DEE-sent.* Another regional (mostly southern) pronunciation which could sound ugly and uneducated. The accent is on the *second* (not first) syllable. It's *dee-SENT.* Also, *dee-SEND* (the verb).

DESIGNATE

This verb means to select, specify, appoint, to give a title to. Be careful to keep the *g* sound; it is *not DES-in-ate* but *DES-ig-nate.*

DESPICABLE

Worthy of being despised, vile. Two reminders: first, it's *des* not *dis;* second, accent on the first syllable is preferred. *DES-pic-uh-bul,* but you do hear *des-PIC-uh-bul.*

DETAIL

Both noun and verb sound far better if the second syllable is accented and the "dee" sound is softened to the *i* sound in *which.* Make it: *duh-TAIL.* See also **DEFENSE** and **DESCENT**.

DETER

To prevent someone from taking some action. Avoid: *dee-TEAR;* it's *dee-TUR* (like *fur*).

DETERIORATE

A good word; it means to decline markedly in quality,

almost to rotting. Watch out for the fact that it has *five* syllables; it is not *duh-TEER-ee-ate*.

Don't use it at all if you don't practice aloud and get it right (*duh-TEER-ee-or-ate*).

DETROIT

Commonly mispronounced. In French, the *de* means *of* (in this case), and *troit* means a narrow place. A glance at the map will show the place between the Great Lakes, and it *is* narrow, hence the French fort there.

Don't offend the Michiganders by making the *de* into *DEE*, or the last syllable into two, *TROY-ut*.

Simply say: *duh-TROIT*, never *DEE-troit*.

DIFFERENT

Three, not two, syllables; *DIF-er-ent*. Avoid *diff-runt* or *diff-rent*.

DIDN'T

Beware *dint*. Also, *shouldn't* has two syllables — not one.

DISCHARGE

This is both a verb (to unload, release, dismiss, etc.) and a noun (an unloading, pouring forth, dismissal). It's somewhat of a fine point, but to sound correct, use *dis-CHARGE* for the verb and *DIS-charge* for the noun.

DISPARATE

This is a useful adjective, if pronounced correctly. It means altogether dissimilar, or completely different in kind. Don't confuse it with *desperate*, which means reckless because of despair or fear.

The word is *DIS-parr-et*.

DISPATCH

As a verb (to send off) or a noun (a message or promptness), it is pronounced with the accent on the *second* syllable. Say: *dis-PATCH*.

DIVORCEE

A divorced woman (not man). Because we have the English word *divorce*, it's easy to forget that **divorcee** is French; hence the *i* is not as in *river,* but a *ee* sound (like *see*). The final *ee* has an accent mark in French (which we don't use in English) that makes the sound *ay* (like *hay*).

Say: *dee-vor-SAY*.

ELEEMOSYNARY

Nonprofit, charitable, giving. Example: The Salvation Army or a church. *EL-uh-MOSS-in-air-ee*.

ELITE

Selected, superior, above the others. Originally French, now fairly common English. Say: *ay-LEET*.

ENCLAVE

An area of land enclosed within a larger area. Preference is *ENN-klave,* but we also hear close to the original French *ON-klave.*

ENCORE

Literally (originally French) *again.* So the orchestra or soloist, to please the audience, plays another short selection. It's *ON-kor.*

ENSEMBLE

Originally French (meaning together) now common English. The first syllable has kept its French connection, while the last two syllables have been modified in English. It means a group (often musicians) or a coordinated costume or suit. Avoid *enn-SEM-bull* and *enn-SAHM-bul.*

Say: *on-SAHM-bul.*

ENTREPRENEUR

A French word, now in ordinary English usage. The person who sets up and operates a business venture or undertaking, usually at some risk.

Two of the syllables can be easily mispronounced. The first syllable should be *on* (not *en*) and the last should be *nur* (like *fur*) not *ewer.*

EPOCH

A period of history, more especially a period of importance. The first choice is *EH-pahk* (the *EH* like the *e* in *pet*), and the second, also acceptable, is *EE-pahk.*

ERA

A specific period of time.

- The year 1920 began the **era** of the American automobile.

The most acceptable (and recommended) pronunciation is *EE-rah*.

ERMINE

The small weasel-like animal and the fur therefrom. Say: *URR-minn* (not *myne*).

ERR/ERROR

Err (verb); to make a mistake. Say *UR* (like *fur*).

Error (noun); a mistake. It's *AIR-rur*.

See **USAGE SECTION**.

ESCHEW

To shun or avoid. It's *ess-SHOO*.

ET CETERA

It means: and so forth. Be careful that the Latin word for *and* is pronounced *et* and not *ex*.

Incidentally, you don't say *and **et cetera*** (and and so forth), a redundancy.

EXACERBATE

It means to make something worse. Say: *eg-ZASS-ur-bate*. Be careful not to confuse it with *exaggerate* or *exasperate*.

EXCAPE

It doesn't exist; it's **es**-*cape*.

EXIT

It's *X-it*; avoid *eggs-zit*.

FEBRUARY

It's the second syllable that is sometimes mangled. It's *FEB-roo-air-ee*. Probably — over time — the *FEB-you* pronunciation will become accepted and, perhaps, even a spelling without the *r*. But, for now, you want to sound correct.

The second syllable is *roo*: practice by saying *FEB-roo-air-ee* aloud several times.

FEMME

See **FOREIGN WORDS**.

FILET

See **FOREIGN WORDS**.

FILM

One syllable; avoid *FILL-um*.

FOLIAGE

This word includes all leaves in general, so it is commonly heard in: the glorious colors of the fall **foliage**. For reasons unknown, one often hears *FOIL-ee-edge* or *FOE-ledge*. Both are wrong. The first syllable rhymes with *toe*.

It's *FOH-lee-edge*.

FOREIGN WORDS

See separate section.

FORTUNATE/FORTUITOUS

Fortunate, say: *FOR-chew-nuht*.

Fortuitous is pronounced *for-too-uh-tus*.

FREQUENT

The verb, meaning to visit often, is accented on the *second* syllable; the adjective, meaning occurring at close intervals, is accented on the *first*.

GALA

As a noun, it means a gay, festive party, or celebration, and as an adjective it means festive or merry, etc. There are several correct pronunciations, but the one that sounds *best* is the one that takes into consideration the French/Spanish root of the word. Therefore: *GAH-lah*.

GARAGE

Beware of making it one syllable: *grahge* (or *grodge*). The *g* in the last syllable slides off like the *g* in beige or the *s* in pleasure. So: *ga-RAHJE*. See **GE=ZH** in **FOREIGN WORDS**.

GENUINE

The real thing. The preferred, and better sounding sound of the last syllable is *in*, to rhyme with tin and win, not with wine. Say: *GEN-yoo-in.*

GIANT

Two syllables; it's *GI-unt.* Avoid *gint.*

GOVERNMENT

Don't forget the *n.* It is neither *guv-er-ment* nor *guv-ment.*

It's *GUV-ern-ment.*

GRAFFITI

Writing or drawings on walls, etc., so as to be visible to the public. The word is plural (singular is **graffito**). Italian, now English. It's *grah-FEET-ee.*

GRIEVOUS

It means causing grief or pain; serious or grave. Watch out that you *don't* put in an extra *i* to make *GREE-vee-us.*

It's *GREE-vus.*

GROCERY

Remember, *three* syllables not two. It's *GROW-sur-ee.*

HARASS

This means to annoy, irritate persistently, or to wear out or exhaust someone. The trick is to put the stress on the first syllable.

Say: *HAR-as* not *ha-RASS*, the *a* as in *apple*.

But in the noun, the preferred pronunciation puts the stress on the second syllable. Say: *ha-RASS-ment.*

HEIGHT (width-length)

It is just plain bad luck, but *width* and *length* end in *h*. Because English is full of irregularities, the one other dimension has no final *h*, and it sounds vastly wrong when so spoken. Practice is needed.

Gimmick to help you remember: **height** has *its* **h** at the beginning, and so doesn't need it at the end.

Another gimmick: **height** rhymes with might and smite; associate **height** with being strong and warlike.

HEINOUS

Extremely wicked or despicable. Say: *HAY-nuss.*

HIATUS

A break or gap in time or other continuous activity, a pause in the flow of events. Say: *hy-ATE-us.*

HORROR

It is not an easy word to pronounce, and, hence, an easy one to say incorrectly. Above all, it's two syllables, and the first syllable is not *har* (like *far*).

Say: *HORE-ruhr.*

HOSPITABLE

Friendly and generous to guests. Akin to *HOS-pit-ul.* Hence, the first syllable accent is preferred. Say: *HOS-pit-uh-bul.*

HOUR

Avoid (in certain areas of the country) *are.* It's: *ow* (as in *how*) *-er.*

HOUSTON

See **HUMID.**

HUGE

See **HUMID.**

HUMID

(Also *huge, Houston, Hugh, humor* and *human*) Even professional radio and television announcers fall into this trap! They probably pull some of you in, too, so beware. These are words that can give you away.

Sorry, but English is full of inconsistencies. In accepted speech we drop the *h* in *honest, heir, herb, hour,* and a few others. But there are other words in which the *h* sound *is* said. Say: *HEW-mid, HEWG,* and the same for the others above.

You would never say *arry* for *Harry* or *urry* for *hurry,* or *ip* for *hip* etc. — that is unless you're a Cockney cab driver!

So why in the world suddenly drop the *h* sound when followed by *u?* There seems to be some black magic about this *u* sound (yet the same sinner would not say *you* for *hew*).

In any case, they are pronounced: *HEW-mid, HEWDGE, HEW-ston, HEW-man* and *hew*.

Practice the *h* sound, realizing that to form it you must blow out a little puff of air. Professor Higgens got Liza to puff a candle in the play *Pygmalion* (later *My Fair Lady.*)

ILLINOIS

The accepted and acceptable last syllable is *oy* (like *boy*).

INCIDENTALLY

It has five syllables; don't confuse it with *incidently* (four syllables), a non-word. It's *in-suh-DENT-uh-lee*.

INFLUENCE

Whether verb or noun, the preferred pronunciation hits the first syllable, Say: *IN-flu-ence*.

INSURANCE

In some rural areas, and in part of the South, the tendency is to accentuate the first syllable. This doesn't sound at all right to the rest of the country. Make it *in-SURE-ance*. Same applies to *in-SURE*.

INTER/INTRO

A dozen commonly used words (*interesting, interrupt*, etc.) begin with these two syllables. The trick is to be sure that the *t* is not lost. It's a lazy speech habit to say *inner-esting*; and it sounds awful.

Also, beware *inner-duce* (meaning *introduce*).

ITALY

Three syllables *IT-uh-lee*.

Also note that Italian is *It-TAL-yen* (not *Eye-TAL-yen*).

KILOMETER

With the USA close to the only nation on earth which does not use (or is switching to) the World (formerly Metric) System, we still find the system gaining ever increasing use here. Three examples: the Olympics, U.S. marathon runs and the one liter bottle.

Because of our long-established habit here of saying *spee-DOM-et-er* and *o-DOM-et-er*, you will hear *kill-OM-et-er*. Yet, if your electrical utility company talked about *kill-O-watts* it would sound absurd to our ears (used to *KILL-o-watts*). What sounds better is the approach taken from science (*MILL-i-meter*, *MILL-i-liter*, etc., and *KILL-o-meter*).

KIOSK

The little stand or booth on the sidewalk or in a park, which contains and shelters a public telephone or offers newspapers, tickets, and other small items for sale. Say: *KEY-ahsk*.

KYOTO

Large Japanese city and long-ago capital. It's two (not three) syllables, evenly accented : *kyo-toe*.

LAMENTABLE

Causing sadness or regret. Because of *la-MENT* (to regret), we do hear *la-MENT-uh-bul,* but *LAM-en-tuh-bul* is preferred.

LARYNX

Commonly called the "voice box," the source of speech in our trachea (windpipe). An extra "n" is often incorrectly added. It's *LAR-inks.*

LENGTH

Rember a *g* sound. So, it's not *lenth* but *LENG-th.* (See **STRENGTH**.)

LIABLE

Pronounced *LYE-uh-bul*, not *LYE-bul.*

LIAISON

Originally French, now English. This is communication between individuals or groups; a close relationship. It's *lee-AY-zon.*

LIBRARY

As with *February*, the *r* in the second syllable is sometimes overlooked. The word comes from the Latin *libraria.*

Say: *LYE-brair-ee.*

LICORICE

The flavor from the root of a plant and the candy therefrom.

The last syllable is *iss* not *rish.*

LINGERIE

See **FOREIGN WORDS**.

LIVED

Here is another inconsistency in English — there are many — with two words spelled the same way but having different meanings, and different pronunciations. *Live* (like *give*) the verb, means to exist or reside: "I *live* on Elm Street."

Live (as in *alive*) as an adjective means having life, or in radio and television jargon, happening at the time of broadcast.

The problem arises with *short* **lived** (something didn't last long). Keep in mind that the **lived** here comes from *life*, so the pronunciation is *short LYE-vd*.

LOATH/LOATHE

The former means unwilling or reluctant.

- The crusty, old-fashioned manager was **loath** to make any changes.

The latter means to detest greatly, to abhor.

- Many people **loathe** turnips and Brussels sprouts, no matter how they're cooked.

The difference in pronunciation is very slight; it is the same kind of change that exists between *bath* and *bathe* and between *lath* (to which plaster is attached) and *lathe* (the machine). So **loath** is *lowth* (rhymes with *both*) while **loathe** starts with *low* but ends with the sliding *th* sound of *bathe* and *lathe*.

LUXURY/LUXURIOUS

There is no *g* sound (it is not *lugg*) in the first syllable.

The meaning is clear, but the wrong impression is conveyed when this noun is used as an adjective (those are **luxury** apartments). The adjective is **luxurious**, so avoid "a luxury apartment." See also **PRESTIGE** in **USAGE**.

MARQUIS/MARQUEE

A nobleman, ranking between duke (above) and an earl. Both the (original) French pronunciation (*mark-KEY*) and the English (*MAR-kwis*) are acceptable, the former is preferred.

Marquee (say *mar-KEY*) is the canopy or structure that extends from a theater, etc., over the main door, usually lighted, and naming the attraction taking place.

MASOCHISM

An abnormal condition in which a person derives satisfaction from abuse, pain or being dominated.

Say: *mass-uh-KIZ-um*.

The adjective is *mass-uh-KIZ-tic*.

MASONRY

Walls, etc., made of stone or brick, constructed with mortar. It's three (not four) syllables. Say: *MAY-sun-ree*, not *MAY-sun-ay-ree*.

MASSAGE

No problem with the meaning, but avoid the *d* sound (not *mas-ODGE*).

The last syllable (like the ending of *garage*) has the *z* sound of *azure* or the *s* in *pleasure*. See **GE=ZH** in **FOREIGN WORDS**.

MATURE

There is no *ch* sound. It is not *ma-CHURE*, but *ma-TURE*. See also **AMATEUR**.

METEOROLOGIST

A person who studies weather, climate, etc. Keep in mind that it contains *meet-ee-or* (three syllables) plus three more (*ol-o-gist*), making six in all. Lazy pronunciation (wrong) comes out: *meet-er-ol-o-gist*.

MINIATURE

It's four (not three) syllables, and the last syllable is *tur* not *chur*. So, avoid *MIN-uh-chur*, it's *MIN-ee-a-tur*.

MIRROR

There are two syllables in this word; it is not *meer*. Yet it is possible to sound too lah-dee-dah by pronouncing the word absolutely correctly, *MEER-rur* (depending, of course, on the educational level of your listener). But, at least, a strong movement away from *meer* and toward the right sound is strongly advised. Then, another time, one can back off just a little when jawing with the boys from shipping.

MISSOURI

The last syllable is "ee" not "uh"; say *miss-OOR-ee.*

MONSTROUS

It means passing all reason or common sense, over-reaching the farthest stretch of the imagination, (a **monstrous** crime). It does not mean enormous or huge.

And it has two, not three, syllables: *MON-strous.*

MOOT/MUTE

Confusion can occur if **moot** is not pronounced correctly. It rhymes exactly with *boot.* It means arguable or debatable. In law it means without legal significance; even though the point has been decided, it is of mere academic interest.

Mute (*MEW-t*) means unable or unwilling to speak; silent.

MORES

The customs, traditions, manners, attitudes and usages of a specific group of people. It's plural, and the most accurate pronunciation is *MAHR-ays,* although *MORE-ays* is also acceptable.

MUSEUM

Be careful to put the accent on the second syllable.

It's *mew-ZEE-um.*

MUTUAL

It's *MYU-choo-al,* not *MYU-chal.*

NAIVE

See **FOREIGN WORDS**.

NAUSEOUS

Foul or evil smelling, sickening, repulsive, causing nausea. Two (not three) syllables; not *NAH-zee-us* but *NAH-zhus.*

NICHE

See **FOREIGN WORDS**.

NUANCE

French, now English, meaning shade, hue, graduation, tinge, slight variation in meaning or quality. It's *NOO-ahns.*

NUCLEAR

The late President Eisenhower (having little or no chemistry or physics background), got part of America off to a bad start in the early '50s by saying *NOO-cue-ler.* The word, of course, is the adjective form of *nucleus,* as in the center of the atom.

It's *NEW-klee-ur.*

OHIO

It ends in "o" not "uh"; say: *oh-HI-oh.*

ONEROUS

Burdensome, troublesome. The preferred pronunciation of the first syllable is like *on* (the preposition; rhymes with *lawn*). Say: *ON-er-us.*

OO

What is referred to here is the *poo* sound in *pool.* Some regional pronunciation tends to substitute a short *u* (as in *pull*) for the *oo* sound. Some common words (and following each one, the pronunciation to be avoided) follow: *tool* (*tull*); *fool* (*full*); *rule* (*rull*); *fuel* (*fyull*).

It may take a little practice to make sure that the *oo* sound is exactly the sound that we were taught, as babies, that cows say (*moo*).

ORANGE

Avoid *ornge* or *arnge* (one syllable, like *hinge*) and avoid *ar-ange.*

Say: *AH-range.*

ORNERY

Describes someone ill-tempered, with a generally irritable disposition.

Pronounce it *OR-ner-ee* (not *on-er-ee*).

OU

We're referring here to the **ou** sound in *out, ouch,* etc. It takes a little effort to say it correctly; the mouth must be opened wide at the beginning, then brought slowly to a close. Otherwise *ouch* becomes *ahtch,* and *out* becomes *aht.*

Others (and how they might also sound — and sound awful) are:

blouse *(blahs),* brown *(brawn),* cloud *(clahd),* clown *(clahn),* down *(dahn),* flour/flower *(flahr),* found *(fahnd),* hound *(hawnd),* hour *(are),* mound *(mahnd),* pound *(pahnd),* round *(rahnd),* town *(tahwn),* etc.

PARTICULAR

It means separate or distinct from others — specific; not general. Beware of two of the four syllables. The first one is *par* not *pah,* and the third one is the subject for difference of opinion among dictionaries and other authorities. One group goes for saying the *u* as a short *uh* sound (the *a* of *about*); the other group goes for the *u* sound of *union.*

What sounds best to the sensitive ear? The *u* sound as in *union.* So it's *par-TICK-u-lur.*

PATIO

No *d* sound; *PAT-ee-oh.* See **PATIO** in **USAGE**.

PECAN

The tree and the nut therefrom. The *preferred* pronunciation is *pee-CAHN* with *a* like father. The *a* (like *man*) is definitely second choice, though you do hear it.

PICTURE/PITCHER

The difference is obvious, but lazy pronunciation sometimes lets the photo come out like the container.

Practice: *PICK-ture*.

PLAZA

A public open area in a city. Both *PLAH-zuh* and *PLA* (like pat)-*zuh* are correct, but the former is preferred.

PRELUDE

Something introductory to a main, more important event; in music, a shorter piece before the main part.

The preferred pronunciation of the first syllable is *pre* (like in *preference*) with the *e* like *men*. In the second syllable, *lyude* is much preferred over *lude*.

PREMISES

Land and the buildings standing on it. Unlike the common *pree* words (premium, premature, etc.), this one rhymes with *hem*; *PREM-iss-ses*.

PREMIERE

See **FOREIGN WORDS**.

PROTEGE

A person whose well being, occupation or career is protected and aided by another, usually influential person. Now fairly common English, the French verb is **proteger** (to protect) and the French pronunciation is universally used (see **GE=ZH** in **FOREIGN WORDS**). It's *PRO-tuh-ZHAY.*

If the person being helped, guided, etc., is female, it's **protegee** (same pronunciation).

QUAY

A reinforced river or harbor bank, or wharf, where ships are loaded/unloaded.

Say: *key.*

QUICHE

See **FOREIGN WORDS**.

RADIATOR/RADIO

It's rare, but when you hear *rad* (like *bad*) you wince; say *ray.*

RAPPORT

A sympathetic, trusting relationship that exists between one person and another (or a group). Originally French, hence *rah-POR,* with the *t* silent.

REALIZE

Beware of *REEL-ize.* It's *REE-uh-lize.*

REALTOR

He/she/they sell real estate, buildings etc. It has *three* syllables: *REE-al-tor.*

RECOGNIZE

Remember — although most of you don't make this error — that the second syllable is *cog* (just like *hog*). So the word is not *REK-kon-ize* but *REK-kog-nize*.

REGIME

The administrative group which is in power; example: the fascist **regime** in control of some nation. Also, the period of such control. The "g" slides off like the "z" in azure. It's: *ray-ZHEEM*. See **GE=ZH** in **FOREIGN WORDS**.

REGULATION

Avoid *reg-uh-LAY-shun;* it's *reg-yew-LAY-shun.*

RELEVANT

Related, connected with, pertinent. Sometimes you may hear *revelant,* which is a non-word.

REMNANT

Something left over. Remember it is two syllables *REM-nant* (*not rem-a-nant*).

RENDEZVOUS

A meeting. It's *RON-day-voo.*

RENEGE

To act against a previous promise or commitment. Say: *ruh-NEEG.*

REPERTOIRE

A group of musical or theatrical works. The second syllable is not *et* but *er;* the last syllable is *twahr. Say: REP-er-twahr.*

RESTAURANT

Watch the pronunciation here (three syllables). Avoid *REST-runt, REST-rahnt* and *RES-turnt.* It may help if you remember that the food served is to *restore* you, and the word comes from the French equivalent for *restorative.* The last syllable has the *a* as *ah,* as *awful.*

It's *REST-or-ahnt* or *REST-uh-rahnt.*

RIDICULOUS

It's the third syllable that sometimes comes out "uh," which is ill-sounding. Say: *ree-DICK-you-luss.*

RINSE

In Appalachia, and in some other parts of the nation, for reasons unknown, this word comes out *rench,* a very ugly sound.

ROOF/ROOT

There is nothing actually wrong with the mid-West, farmer-style pronunciation of these words to rhyme with *muff* and *rut.* But the fact is that the standard, urban, always acceptable pronunciation is to give the *oo* sound of *moo* or *through.* It makes a better impression.

ROUTE/ROUT

Meaning a particular way or path for travel.

- The best **route** to Chicago is to take the XYZ turnpike.

- There was an accident on **Route** 79.

It is the same in French or English; it rhymes with *boot.*

A **rout** (rhymes with about) is the disorderly retreat of an army, or a crushing 60-10 football score.

Keeping separate the two words, which differ widely in meaning, is a nice and useful distinction.

SABOTEUR

One who secretly damages some property or operation. The last syllable rhymes with *fur* not *pure.* Say: *sah-bah-TUR.*

SANDWICH

The word has a *d.* No one would ever say, "kids love to play in the *san*" or "in the *sam*." But he might jar your ears (and your opinion of him) by saying *san-wich* or — ouch — *sam-ich.*

SAUCE

See **FOREIGN WORDS**.

SAUTERNE

See **MENU** in **FOREIGN WORDS**.

SAYS/SEZ

English is full of odd-ball exceptions. **Say** is the same in the present tense in every form except the third person singular.

- He **says** it isn't so.

The **says**, centuries ago, was pronounced *sayz* but has since gone to the now usual and acceptable *sez*.

But be careful not to use **says** for anything expect *he*, *she*, or *it;* never use it for *I*, *you*, *we* or *they*.

SCHISM

A division or splitting. The preferred pronunciation is *SIZZ-em*. How to remember? In a sense, the *ch* is silent, as is the *c* in *scissors* (which cut, split or divide).

SEMI

Say: *SEM-ee,* also see **USAGE** listing.

SIGNIFICANT/SIGNIFY

Don't forget the "g" It's **sig** not *sin*. Say: *sig-NIF-eh-cant.*

SLURVIAN

Some years ago a humorous magazine editor created this imaginary foreign language. Poking fun at mistakes and strange habits can be helpful in calling our attention to our habitual errors.

In **Slurvian** the speaker sounds as if his mouth is full of marbles, blurring all the sounds. For example, the toothpaste commercial strikes the ear as:

- I got feur caties sinz I swisha cress. (Translation: I have fewer cavities since I switched to Crest.)

Occasionally two **Slurvians** will meet on the street:

- Jeet yet? (Did you eat yet?)

- No. Joo? (No. Did you?)

Diction is the act of (a) choosing which words to say, and (b) saying them clearly. Listening to yourself speak, as well as listening to others, will help you develop attractive and impressive speech habits.

STRENGTH

Remember that there is a *g* sound (like *strong*). So it is not *stren-th* but *STRENG-th*. (See also **LENGTH**.)

SUBSIDIARY

The third syllable is *ee*; it's *sub-SID-ee-ary*, not *sub-SID-u-ary*.

SUITE/SUIT

The former designates two or more things in a series, usually connected; hence, the rooms of an office or hotel **suite**.

Pronounced: *sweet.*

Suit (rhymes with *toot*) is the great grandson of **suite**. It has lost its French Connection completely, except for the fact that the jacket and trousers (or skirt) do follow one another in fabric, color, etc., and hence are linked (and worn) together.

SUPERINTENDENT

Five syllables; trick to remember: the "super" "intends" to oversee things. Say: *soo-per-in-TEND-ent.*

TEMPERAMENT

It's *four* syllables (remember the *a*). *TEM-pur-uh-ment.*

THEATER

An apology to the overwhelming majority who pronounce this correctly, but a caution to the others. Saying *thee-ATE-ur* sounds very hick, and is to be avoided at all costs. It's *THEE-uh-tur.*

TITANIC

The ancient Greek god Titan gave rise to "a titan," i.e., a person of huge size, strength or accomplishment. The adjective has two (not three) *t's.*

Because of many familiar words ending in *tic:* (Atlantic, arctic, etc.), there is a tendency to err (not *error*) by saying "titantic."

It's *tie-TAN-ick.*

TOKYO

Japan's capital. It's two (not three) syllables, equally accented: *toe-kyo.*

TOWEL

This word, like *mirror*, has *two* syllables, and requires some effort of mouth and tongue to obtain a reasonably well-sounding result. The first syllable rhymes with *how*. It's *TOW-uhl*.

TOYOTA

Japanese words accent all syllables with almost identical stress, unlike English. This guide does not expect many readers to follow this rule (the TV commercials say *toy-OH-tah*), but you may find it fun to be correct.

It's *toe-yoe-tah*.

UNDER

Don't fail to pronounce the "d"; otherwise, your listener will hear "unner." This applies, of course, also to words beginning with under (like *understand*, etc.).

VEGETABLE

Remember, there are four syllables; the second syllable tends to be forgotten; it's *VEG-uh-tuh-bull*.

VETERAN

It's three syllables; avoid *VET-run*.

VICE VERSA

Latin; the reversal of the meaning or of the order of things. Say: *VYS-uh VURS-uh*.

VOWELS

There are regions of the country in which certain vowel sounds soften into a form of Southern accent. The *a*, as in *hay,* the *e* sound as in *bee,* and the *i* as in *mile* become very short vowel sounds.

The long *a* sound (in *pail, sail, mail*) may turn out much like *el.* Not only does this sound awful, but it may lead to momentary confusion when, for example, *tale* sounds like *tell.*

The long *e* sound (in *steel, peel*) raises the same problems. So *steel* becomes *still, peel* becomes *pill* and *wheel* becomes *will.*

The long *i* sound (in *mile* and *tile*) should be a pure *eye* sound or else you may be confusing your listener when you mention a *mahl* (mile) or *tahl* (tile) or *fahl* (file).

Only southwest, millionaire oil barons can get away with these sounds.

VOYEUR

French, now fairly common English; literally one who sees. Modern meaning is toward one who *secretly* sees, i.e., peeks or spies. It's: *voy-ERR* (like *fur*).

"W"

The twenty-third letter. Keep in mind its origin: double *u.* The pitfalls are *double-yuh* and *dub-uh-yuh.*

It's: *double-yew.*

WASH

Be sure it's *wahsh* and has no *r* sound; in some parts of the country, it comes out *warsh* (as in *Warshington*) and sounds awful.

WREAK

This old, almost archaic word means to inflict venge-ance on somebody or to express anger. Say *reek* (like *speak*).

Part 3
Foreign Words

The following section on foreign words is here because English is an unequalled borrower from other languages — and has been for centuries. So, to varying degrees, these words may be heard in conversation. Their meaning and their pronunciation is, understandably, a bit more difficult than the long-established "English" words. As a result, they may require a little extra practice so the person talking feels comfortable.

Note: the words selected for this section have been adopted into English from six other languages. Following each word is a letter indicating that language: the letter code is: F (French), G (German), I (Italian), L (Latin), S (Spanish) and Y (Yiddish). Some words are equally at home in English and their original language; these are marked — as an example — (E) (F).

ACCOUTERMENT (F)

Something added in equipment or apparel, or anything added, more or less, for show. It's *ah-COOO-tur-mahnt.*

ADIOS (S)

Good-bye. It's literally "to God." *Say: ah-DEE-ose.*

ADOBE (S)

A brick baked in the sun; also, the clay so used and a structure made from such bricks. Say: A*h-DOE-bee.*

AFICIONADO (S)

It means an admirer or enthusiastic follower.

It's *ah-feesh-ee-uh-NAH-doe.*

A LA CARTE (F)

Literally, from (or on) the card (menu). Hence, one selects the desired items one by one. It's *ah-lah-cart.*

AMBIANCE (F)

The general atmosphere or mood of a place. It's *AM-bee-ons.*

AU (F)

To or **with.** Say: *oh.*

AVANT-GARDE (F)

This applies to those who are leaders, innovators, out in front, ahead of the pack, especially in the arts. Or, as an adjective, having those qualities. It's *ah-vahn-GARD.*

BIDET (E) (F)

The porcelain fixture for washing, found on the floor in hotel (and some private) bathrooms, largely in Europe. Say: *BEE-day.*

BOU (E) (F)

Many French words beginning with these letters are now fairly commonly used in English. The trick to

remember is that **bou** is pronounced *boo*. Some
examples: boucle, boudoir, bouffant, bouillabaisse,
bouillon, boulevard, bouquet, bourgeois, Bougogne,
boutonniere, etc.

BOUQUET (E) (F)

The first syllable is *boo*. So: *boo-KAY*.

BOUTIQUE (E) (F)

A small shop. The *bou* is the same one (like *booth*) we
found in *bouquet*. It's *boo-TEEK*.

BOUTONNIERE (E) (F)

A little flower (or a tiny group of them) worn on the
lapel or in a button hole there. It's *boo-tun-YAIR*.

BRAVADO (S)

Show-off bravery; an ostentatious or boastful act. Say:
brah-VAH-doe.

BUFFET (E) (F)

Means either the piece of furniture in the dining room,
or, by extension, a style of serving a meal in which
each guest serves himself (not *them*self) from the
buffet (or sideboard, table, etc.).

People get the last syllable right because we all know
how to say Chevrolet (a *French* auto pioneer, by the
way). But the first syllable is like *boo* not like *buff*.
Actually the *u* sound in French doesn't have an exact
English equivalent. If you're brave, purse your lips as
though to whistle and then say the *boo* part.

BURRITO (S)

Little mule. *BOOR-EET-oh.*

CACHET (F)

An individual sign, symbol or mark. Now extended to mean a certain individual aura or image. It's *kah-SHAY.*

CAUSE CELEBRE (F)

A legal case, or other issue, arousing considerable public interest, debate and argument. Say: *cohz say-LEB-ruh.*

CHAISE LONGUE (E) (F)

French for *long chair* and widely misunderstood and mispronounced. **Chaise** is simply *chair,* remembering that the *ch* is *sh* as is Chevrolet, the French automobile pioneer; so: *shayz.* The larger and extremely ill-sounding problem comes from the adjective *long* (spelled the same as in English), if modifying a masculine word, and **longue** (same pronunciation) for a feminine word.

Bad luck; **chaise** is feminine so the adjective is **longue**; it *follows* the noun, common in French, unusual in English.

Worse luck; **longue** has the same six letters as the common, unrelated English word *lounge* (verb: to lie aimlessly around; noun: a bar or a rest room, lavatory or toilet in a public place, such as a theater, etc.).

So well-meaning, unknowing speakers confuse the words and use *lounge* when they obviously mean **longue** (long). Say: *shayz long*.

CHEZ (F)

At the home (place) of. So "**chez** Marie" is "Mary's place (home)." Say: *shay*. If a vowel follows **chez**, pronounce the "z." Example: **chez** Andre. Say: *shaz-ON-dray*.

CHIC (E) (F)

In style, fashionable, appealing to very modern taste. The *i* in French is always *ee* (*Gigi, Mimi*). Say: *sheek*.

CLICHE (E) (F)

Something said (or done) too often, repeated; worn out; over used. The *i* is *ee*, so avoid *klish-ay*; say: *KLEE-shay*.

CLIQUE (E) (F)

A tight, usually small, group of followers or persons with a cause in common. Say: *kleek*.

COMMUNIQUE (F)

An official announcement or letter to be made public. It's *cuh-MYOON-eh-KAY*.

CONCIERGE (E) (F)

The person in the hotel reception area who handles

special requests, tickets, transportation and other matters needed by guests. It's *kohn-see-AIRGE*. The *ge* slides off like the end of garage. See also **GE=ZH**.

COUP D'ETAT (F)

The **coup** means quick stroke or blow — in other words a sudden, decisive act. **Etat** means the state (i.e., government). Hence, it's a sudden rebellion which brings into power a new ruler. Often used simply as **coup**.

Say: *koo-day-tah*.

COUPE (E) (F)

Now common English, though French. The verb is *couper* (*koop-AY*) to cut or cut off. So this form of the verb describes something that has been cut off or shortened. So the (formerly) shorter version of a sedan, with two doors instead of four, is a "cut off" model. The *e* in French has a mark making it say *ay*. Say: *koop-AY*, although you do hear *koop*.

There *is* a French word, coupe (*koop*) meaning *cup*. One common use applies to a dessert in a rather tall glass (originally a cup) filled with various ice creams, sherbets, syrups, fruit, etc. They are usually given fancy names like **Coupe** St. Jacques, etc.

CROISSANT (E) (F)

It means *crescent* (half moon) or *crescent shaped*. Hence, it is applied to the *c* shaped roll of leavened dough or pastry.

Say: *KRWAH-sahn* (the *t* is silent).

CUISINE (E) (F)

Now almost common English, it means (literally) *kitchen* but has come to mean the style of cooking. So we hear phrases like Italian **cuisine**. It has retained its French root, hence it's *kwee (not quiss)-ZEEN.*

DECOR (F)

The interior style and decoration of fabrics, furniture, etc. In French, the *e* has a mark making it say *ay* and this pronunciation has remained. It's *day-KOR.*

DE RIGEUR (F)

Something or some act "required" by social customs or fashion; a social "necessity." Say: *duh ree-GURR* (rhymes with fur).

DEJA VU (F)

Literal French *already seen.* The *de* is *day*; the *j* is the *z* sound of azure or the *s* in pleasure; the *a* is, as always, *ah*, the *vu* is close to *voo*; avoid *vue*. So, *DAY-zhah voo.*

See also **GE=ZH**.

DESPERADO (S)

A hopeless, desperate person or outlaw. Say: *des-puh-RAH-doe.*

DEVOTEE (E) (F)

Someone literally devoted to a cause or particular interest. Example: a **devotee** of opera or jazz or Mexican food. Say: *dev-oh-TAY.*

DISCOTHEQUE (E) (F)

A phonograph record in French is a *disc.* The word for library is *bibliotheque.* So when some nightclub owner in Paris, decades ago, put in stacks of records and got a lot of the young dancing, he coined the combination of *disc* plus *theque.* The letter *i* is always *ee* (Mimi). Hence: *DEES-ko-tek.*

DIVORCEE (E) (F)

A divorced woman (not man). Because we have the English word *divorce,* it's easy to forget that **divorcee** is French; hence the *i* is not as in river, but a *ee* sound (like see). Say: *dee-vor-SAY.*

DOUBLE ENTENDRE (F)

Literally double heard or understood, and today referring to a word or phrase which has an obvious, and also a subtle, *second* meaning (often on the risque (see) side). Say: *DOOB-luh on-TAHND-ruh.*

ELITE (E) (F)

Selected; superior; above the others. Originally French, now fairly common English. Say: *ay-LEET.*

ENTREE (E) (F)

It means admittance or introduction (the verb is *entrer,* to enter).

It formerly meant a dish served in a formal dinner, just before (introduction to) the main course. It has now come to mean the main course of an ordinary dinner.

Say: *ON-tray* (not *EN-tray*).

ERGO (L)

Therefore. Say: *UR-go.*

FAIT ACCOMPLI (F)

A "done deal" or already accomplished deed or fact beyond question. Say: *fate ah-kohm-PLEE.*

FAUX (F)

False, fake, pretend, as beads (on a necklace) made to look like pearls. Say: *foe.*

FAUX PAS (F)

Literally, "false step," hence error, oversight. Say: *foe pah.*

FEMME (F)

As is widely known, it means *woman* or *wife*. It often appears in the phrase "cherchez la **femme**" (*SHAIR-shay lah fawm*) meaning search for a (or some) woman. **Femme** rhymes with palm not with hem.

FEMME FATALE (F)

Literally "fatal woman" in French; having an unusually attractive, seductive and possible dangerous charm. It's *fawm fah-TAHL.*

FIANCE/FIANCEE (E) (F)

The man or woman to whom someone is engaged to be married. The man has one *e;* the woman, two. The pronunciation is the same: *fee-ahn say.*

FICHE (E) (F)

Although French, the word is rapidly becoming English, especially in the term *microfiche*. It means *leaf* (of a book) or *page*. Photography makes possible placing large amounts of legible information on a sheet of film which is then put into a magnifier and read by the user. It rhymes with **niche** (see) and *leash*. Say: *feesh*.

FIESTA (S)

A party; *fee-YEH-stah.*

FORTE (E) (F)

A notable or particular skill or strength possessed by someone. In French, the *e* is silent; so it's *FORT.* (In *music* terms, where Italian is almost universally used, playing loudly is playing **forte**, and it's *for-TAY.*)

Remember: *FORT.* Avoiding the hundred worst speech boo-boos can be your **forte**.

GE=ZH (F)

The sound of this ending (occasionally the beginning) of several French words is a little difficult because we have in English no exact duplicate. We do have words from French, now frequently used in English, and the ending sound of them will be helpful to the reader to get the *idea*: garage, barrage, beige, concierge, corsage, rouge, massage, etc.

We show this in the book as *ZH.* It slides off like the *z* in *azure* or the *s* in *pleasure*.

French words beginning with *j* have the same sliding *ZH* sound (not the hard *j* of *jump*).

GOURMET (E) (F)

An expert in the field of fine food and drink. It is not *gore* but *goor* (like *too*). So: *goor-may*.

See also **BOU**.

By the way, a person who takes a delight in eating well, and does so frequently, is a gourmand (*goor-mahnd*).

GRAND PRIX (F)

Largest prize; also, **prix** can mean *price*. Say: *grah(n) pree*. The *n* is very slightly heard.

HASTA LA VISTA (S)

The **hasta** means until, and the **vista** indicates the sight of someone. So, "see you in the future" or "see you soon" or even "so long." It's *AH-stah lah BEE-stah*.

IPSO FACTO (L)

By the very fact itself. It's *IP-so FACT-toe*.

LA DOLCE VITA (I)

The "sweet" (good, luxurious, pleasurable) life. Say: *lah-DOLE-chay VEE-tah*.

LARGESS (F)

It means generosity, liberal in giving. The *g* has the sound (represented as *GH=ZH*) of the *z* in azure or the *s* in pleasure; *lar-GH-ZHESS*.

LINGERIE (E) (F)

Womens' underwear, etc. The word is almost universally mispronounced. Be the first on your block to get it approximately right! The first syllable is the hardest one to imitate in English. It's the *an* of *angle,* but said as if the nose were stopped up, so there is almost no *n* sound. It is not lawn.

The second syllable is *jair,* with the *j* sounding like the *s* in *measure,* not the *j* in *jump;* the *e* sounds ay.

The last syllable is simply ee as in *bee.* It is not ay (like *hay*).

Say: *lan-zhair-ee.*

LIQUEUR (E) (F)

This is the sweet after-dinner alcoholic drink, also called a cordial. It is pronounced *lee-KUR;* the second syllable is *not* pronounced *cure.*

LOGE (F)

A box in a theater, usually above the ground floor level, or at either side. Also, the front seat area in the first mezzanine (first balcony).

It's: *lohzh;* the *j* slides off and sounds like the *z* in *azure,* the s in *pleasure,* or the end of *garage.*

See also **GE=ZH**.

MAITRE D'HOTEL (E) (F)

This is the head steward, butler, headwaiter, proprietor, boss. The *re* is a bit difficult for those inexperienced in French; it's a *very* quiet (nearly silent) *ruh.* But perhaps the best you'll be able to do is a standard *ur* sound, so it ends up *MAY-tur* rather than the correct *MAY-truh*.

The last part is easy: *doe-tell*.

There is a wide misunderstanding about the word *hotel* in this phrase. To Americans, it has only one obvious meaning, but in reality, it also means large (or town) house, or important public building. For example, "Hotel de Ville" (city) is the city hall, where the administration presides; and "Hotel Dieu" (God) is a hospice or public building offering shelter and often medical aid to the destitute or ill, usually run by a religious order.

Because of this original meaning (from which our modern, conventional hotel has evolved), we might shy from using the **d'Hotel** when we're speaking of the headwaiter in a restaurant — even though it is correct.

And that results in the ill-sounding and jarring **maitre d** (*MAY-tur dee*). We advise strongly against such use, and suggest either the full phrase or, simply, head-waiter.

MANANA (S)

Tomorrow — or sometime after that. *Mahn-YAHN-uh.*

MAUVE (F)

This is the purple or violet color. It is pronounced to rhyme with *cove* or *trove*.

MELEE (F)

Originally, a brawling, hand-to-hand fight; now, a pushing, congested, crowding together. The preferred pronunciation is the French style: *MAY-lay.*

MENU (E) (F)

(Say: *may-new* or *men-yew*). French cuisine is so widely practiced in the U.S. that it becomes very likely to encounter a complete menu, or at least several French words, on a mixed menu. So, these words could prove helpful.

ASPERGE	asparagus *as-PAIRZH* (the *g* like the end of *garage*)
AGNEAU	lamb *ahn-yoe*
A LA CARTE	**La carte** is the menu so the phrase means from (or on) the menu. Say: *ah-lah-cart.*
ARTICHAUT	artichoke *ART-ee-show* FOND D'ARTICHAUTS: heart (bottom) of the artichoke.
AUBERGINE	eggplant *oh-bair-jeen*; the *j* is like the *z* in azure. See **GE=ZH**
AU GRATIN	Crusted or topped with browned crumbs, butter and often cheese. It's *oh GRAW-ta(n).* The *AU* is *oh.*
AU JUS	With (its own) juice. So the roast of beef will often be served with the juice from the roasting pan. Remember that the **au** means *with*, so "*with* **au jus**" does not make sense. Say: *oh zew*, the *z* having the **GE=ZH** sound (see).
BEURRE	butter *burr*

MENU (continued)

BISQUE	A light cream soup, often made from seafood. Exactly rhymes with *risk* in America — *beesk* in French.
BOEUF	beef *buhf*, with a slight *ee* sound in the *u*
BOUILLABAISSE	A hearty fish stew *BOO-ee-yuh-bayz*
BOURGUIGNON	In the style of Burgundy (as in Bouef Bourguignon: beef stew in red wine, bacon, onion, mushrooms) Say: *BOOR-geen-yo(n)*; (the *g* as in *go*)
CANAPE	A bit of bread or toast on which has been placed a small piece of fish, meat or cheese. Say: *can-uh-PAY*.
CHAMPIGNON	mushroom *shahm-PEEN-yo(n)* the final *n* is almost silent and through the nose; you'll see this several places in this section.
CHOU-FLEUR	cauliflower *shoo-flur*
CHOUCROUTE	sauerkraut *shoo-krewt*
CITRON	lemon *SEE-tron*
CREME de MENTHE	The sweet, mint-flavored liqueur; the literal translation from French is *cream* of *mint,* but the **creme** is *krem* not cream. **Menthe** is *mahnth* and the **de** is a hardly-heard *duh*.
CREPE	A very thin pancake, often doused with flavorings to make a fancy dessert. It's pronounced *krape* (like *ape*).

MENU (continued)

CREVETTE   shrimp   *crev-ETT*

DEMI TASSE   half (coffee)
                 cup   *DEM-ee tahs*

ENDIVE   endive   American: *ENN-dive* but
                           we also hear French
                           ON-deev

EPINARD   spinach   *ay-peen-AR*

FARCI   stuffed   *far-CEE*

FILET MIGNON We all understand that filet is that
tender part of a beef steak. Some-
times we forget about the letter *i* in
French words; we should rely on our
girl friends — Gigi, Mimi, and Fifi —
to remind us that *i* is pronounced *ee*
(as in *see*). So it's *fee-LAY*. The
mignon (meaning small) is *mean-
yo(n)*, with the final *on* as described
under **-ON** (see).

                   FEE-lay meen-YON.

FINE HERBES herbs for
                 seasoning *feen-airb*

FRAISE   strawberry *frayz*

FROMAGE   cheese   *froh-mahge* (the *g* like
                           the end of *garage*)
                           See **GE=ZH**

FRAMBOISE   raspberry *frahm-bwahz*

GATEAU   cake   *gah-toe*

MENU *(continued)*

GIGOT   leg   *JEE-go* (the *j* is like *z* sound in *azure*)
See **GE=ZH**

GRUYERE   That delicious cheese; it's *grew-yair.*

HARICOTS   beans   *ahr-ee-coe*

HARICOTS VERTS
green beans
ahr-ee-coe vair

HORS D'OEUVRES
The small appetizers or canapes served with cocktails or before a meal. Incidentally **hors** means *outside,* the **d'** means *of,* and **oeuvre** means *main work* (the main course). As the words came to be used in America, an *s* was stuck on the end of **oeuvre** because we wanted to make it plural, to show that several kinds of appetizers were served. The mistake has stuck in print, but because the phrase is French, the final *s* is silent. So it's, "they served several tasty *or-DURVE.*"

HOMARD   lobster   *oh-MAR*

JAMBON   ham   *jham-boh(n)* (the *j* is like the *z* sound in azure) See **GE=ZH**

JOUR   Literally, French for *day* (journal, journey, etc.). We see it in "soupe du **jour**", etc. The *j* is not the *j* of *jump* but the ***GE=ZH*** sound (see). So: *zhour.*

MENU (continued)

JUS

The natural juice that is found in the pan after roasting meat. The *j* sound is one of those for which there is no exact equivalent in English. It is not the *j* of *jump*; it is (in French) always the soft *g* sound as the *s* in "measure" or the *z* in *azure*. See **GE=ZH**. The *s* is silent, so the us is approximately oo. Say: *ZZEW*.

You see *au **jus***, meaning with its own juice. The *au* is *oh*.

LEGUME   vegetable *lay-goom*

NICOISE   as in **salade nicoise**; contains (usually): tuna, anchovies, tomatoes, potatoes, green beans, hard boiled egg and lettuce. *NEES-wahz*

PATE   a smooth paste, almost always of meat, and usually eaten on crackers, toast, etc. Say: *PAH-tay*.

POMME DE TERRE

apple of the earth;
potato   *pohm-duh-tair*

PORC   pork   *por*

POTAGE   thick soup *poh-tahge*
                            See *GE=ZH*

POULET   chicken   *pool-LAY*
also
POULARDE,   *poo-LARD,*
CAPON,   *kahp-O(N),*
COQ,   *coke,*
VOLLAILLE   *vohl-AY*

MENU *(continued)*

RAGOUT	meat/vegetable stew	*ra-GOO* — the *a* like *apple*
RIZ	rice	*ree*
ROTI	roasted	*roe-TEE*
SAUMON	salmon	*soe-moh(n)*
TOURNEDOS	a very small beefsteak	*TOURN-uh-doh*
VEAU	veal	*voe*
VIN	wine	*va(n)* — the *a* like *apple*

ALSACE	*al-sass*
ANJOU	*ahn-zhoo*
BEAUJOLAIS	*boe-zho-lay* See **GE=ZH**
BEAUNE	*bone*
BORDEAUX	*bor-doe*
BOURGOGNE	*boor-GOYNE*
CABERNET	*cah-bare-NAY*
CHABLIS	*shah-BLEE*
CHAMBERTIN	*shah-bare-TA(N)* — the *a* like *apple*
CHARDONNAY	*shar-dun-AY*
CHENIN	*SHEH-na(n)* — the *a* like *apple*
GAMAY	*gah-MAY*
GRAVES	*grahv*
GRENACHE	*gruh-NAHSE*
MACON	*may-so(n)*
MEDOC	*MAY-dok*
MERLOT	*MAIR-low*
MONTRACHET	*mohn-rah-SHAY*

MENU (continued)

MOUTON CADET	*moo-tah(n) cah-day*
MUSCADELLE	*MOOS-kah-DELL*
MUSCADET	*MOOS-kah-DAY*
PINOT	*PEE-noe*
POMMARD	*poe-MAR*
POUILLY FUISSE	*poo-YEE FWEEZ-ay*
POUILLY FUME	*poo-YEE FOO-may*
PULIGNY	*pool-een-YEE*
RIESLING	*reez-ling*
SAINT	*sa(n)* — the *a* like apple
SAINTE	*saynt*
SAUTERNE	*soe-TURN*
SAUVIGNON	*SOE-vee-YO(N)*
VOUVRAY	*voo-VRAY*
Also useful:	
BLANC	*blah(nk)*
BLANCHE	*blahnshe*
ROUGE	*roozh*
	See **GE=ZH**
NOIR	*nwahr*
VILLAGE(S)	*vee-LAHGE*
	See **GE=ZH**

MESA (S)

Table; also tableland (takes table shape). *MAY-sah.*

MESQUITE (S)

Dry tumbleweed. *MESS-keet.*

MILIEU (F)

An environment or a locale. Because it's French, the *i*, as always, is said *ee.* Say: *meel-YEW.*

NAIVE (E) (F)

This word, meaning simple, innocent, unsophisticated, is both French and English and is pronounced the same in both. Say: *nah-EVE.*

NICHE (E) (F)

Originally, a depression or recess in the wall usually to hold a small statue or other object. Now it has come to mean a particular place — usually a suitable and fitting one.

- He moved through several jobs in the company and finally found his **niche**.

There is no *t* sound is the word, and the *i* (since the word is from French) is pronounced *ee.* Say it like *leash.*

NON SEQUITOR (L)

You'll recognize the source of our word *sequence* (one thing, following another). The phrase means "it does not follow." So, if someone says, "being tall and dark, he was fond of music," you'll understand "not following." Say: *nahn SEK-quit-or.*

NOUVEAU RICHE (F)

Literally *new rich,* meaning relatively newly arrived into the big bucks scene. By extension, it has come to mean wealthy, but not sophisticated, not cultured or refined.

Say: *noo-voe-REASH*; the *reash* rhymes with *quiche* in French or *leash* in English.

-ON

You've notice this as the ending syllable of several words in this section (mignon, bourguignon, champignon, citron, jambon, capon, saumon, etc.) It has the grunt-like sound of the **on** in *bronco* or *honk,* but said with the nose closed, and the merest *hint* of an *n* sound at the end.

PAR EXCELLENCE (F)

The very best; preeminent. Say: PAR (like far) -ex-sell-AHNCE.

PASSE (F)

Out of date, outmoded. From French (meaning past) where the *a* would be *ah,* but Anglicized today to the *a* of *pat.* The *e* has retained the sound from French where a mark makes it say *ay.* So, *pa-SAY* or *pah-SAY.*

PER SE (L)

The **per** means in, of or by, and the **se** means itself. Say: *purr say* (although *see* is also correct, but rare).

PIECE DE RESISTANCE (F)

The main dish in a meal, and also the highest point or most outstanding feature of a program or series.

It's *pee-ess duh ray-ZEEZ-tahns.* The last syllable is a close rhyme to the British style of pronouncing *dance.*

PIQUE(F)

A fabric with a raised or relief pattern. It keeps its French pronunciation: *pee-KAY.* When it becomes a verb, it becomes English (to simulate or arouse) and becomes *peek*.

PORTE-COCHERE (E) (F)

Literally, door for coaches. Most commonly today, a sort of porch roof near a doorway, projecting out over a driveway, to provide shelter for those entering or leaving vehicles.

Say: *port coe-SHARE*.

POTPOURRI (F)

A mixture of odd things; an unusual put-together. It's *poh-poor-EE*.

PREMIERE (E) (F)

As a noun, it means the first presentation of a play or movie. It is often mispronounced as *pree-MEER*. It should be three syllables, and the first syllable should be more like *prem* (rhymes with *stem*).

Say: *prem-ee-yair*

Though fairly widely used as a verb, this use causes many a wince and should be avoided.

- (incorrect) The movie will **premier** next week.

- (correct) The movie will open next week.

- (correct) The **premiere** of the movie will be next week.

PRIX FIXE (F)

On a menu, or on a sign outside a restaurant, you'll see these words followed by a price. The meal shown is offered, complete, for the fixed price shown.

Say: *pree-feeks*.

QUICHE (E) (F)

The cheese pie. It's *KEY-sh*. Rhymes with leash, as (not *like*) is used on a dog.

RAISON D'ETRE (F)

The **raison** means reason, motive, or grounds for; the **etre** means to be (or being), to exist. Therefore, the whole phrase means reason to exist, justification of something.

The *on* is a very short, hardly heard *n* grunt with the nose stopped up. The final *re* is a very small, hardly heard *r* sound.

Say: *RAYS-ahn DAYT-ruh*.

RISQUE (E) (F)

A joke or remark that is just a little bit off color, suggestive, or indelicate.

- The **risque** joke was more suitable for the men's locker room than for the formal dining room.

Say: *rees-KAY*, to be accurate, though *ris-KAY* is more commonly heard.

RODEO (S)

Small, circular amphitheater. *ROE-dee-oh*.

SALON (E) (F)

Literally a room (other than a bedroom), but expanded to mean a large enclosed area where certain business activities take place (hair styling, women's high-fashion clothing).

The *a* is *ah* as in *awful.* The last syllable has now become Anglicized and *on* (like the preposition meaning on top of) is accepted.

SALSA (S)

Sauce. *SAHL-suh.*

SAUCE (E) (F)

Same word in English and French, same meaning. But on menus, it's usual to see **sauce** Hollandaise or **sauce** Bernaise, etc. This is French, and quite different from the English sauce, *SAWSS.*

In French **sauce**, you'll see your friend *AU* (see); it's pronounced *oh.*

So: *SOHZ.*

Incidentally, the "H" of *Hollandaise* is silent; the "Ber" of *Bernaise* is "bare."

SAUTE (E) (F)

Cooked in a skillet or frying pan, usually in butter. You'll see your friend *AU* again. It's *soe-tay.*

Because it means *cooked*, it's not correct to say *saut<u>ed</u>* (the past tense is already built into the word). But if you are more comfortable using it incorrectly, then at least you won't be saying **saw**-*tayed.*

SIERRA (S)

Saw; mountain range. *See-AIR-uh.*

SOIREE (F)

A party or reception in the evening. The French for evening is *soir.* It's *swah-RAY.*

TABLE D'HOTE (F)

This is the menu for a meal that has been pre-selected by the host (*hote*: innkeeper, restaurateur, etc.) as opposed to selections made one by one by the diner, from a menu (*a la carte*) (see).

Say: *tah-bull dote.*

TRES CHIC (F)

Very "in," i.e., in style, in favor, in vogue. Say: *tray sheek.*

VAUDEVILLE (F)

A theatrical program of songs, dances, comedy and variety acts, popular in the first third of this century. In the first syllable is seen an old friend (au pronounced oh). Say: *VODE-vill.*

VERBOTEN (G)

Forbidden, prohibited. It has retained its German sound. Say: *fair-BOH-tun.*

VERITE (F)

True, real. You see it in the phrase *cinema VERITE,* meaning that the movie is realistic, true to life. It keeps it's French pronunciation, in which both "e's" have an *ay* sound. Say: *VARE-it-tay.*

VICHYSSOISE (E) (F)

That delicious potato soup seen often on menus and so often murdered in pronunciation.

The first syllable is simply *veesh* (not like wish). The "y" is *ee* (like bee). People get the "soi" (*swah*) about right, but fail to do the *z* sound at the very end.

Thus: *veesh-ee-swahz.*

VIGNETTE (E) (F)

French, but becoming increasingly English. A small design or portrait, and by extension, a brief intimate literary work. It's *veen-yet.*

VIS-A-VIS (F)

One word for *face* in French is *visage*, and this **vis** is a shortened form. In other words, face-to-face or opposite, against, in relation to, etc.

Say: *veez-ah-vee.*

Part 4
Now Test Yourself

Of course, all the points raised in this guide could not be included in a brief quiz. But this little story will illustrate a few, and will show how *easy* it is to sound bad — and to do so *often*. That's a good incentive to improve.

It is important to read this following story *aloud*, and *preferably* with someone else listening. We learn how things sound by *hearing* them said — properly or poorly. Be brave and don't cheat; read it aloud first, *then* score yourself.

Each line is numbered. Following the story, there is a guide (page 195) which relates the line numbers (in which there *may* be one or two errors) to the *page number* in the book which deals with that particular problem.

1   The camping trip was to begin the next morning.

2   "I'm not sure we ought to be taking the boys along
3   with us," said Bill. "Just between you and I, this could
4   be a little bit too rough of a trip— maybe a gentler one
5   would of been a smarter choice."

6   "Nah," replied Bob impatiently, "I'm anxious to get
7   going! That 8:00 AM in the morning can't get here
8   soon enough to suit me!"

9   "Well," Bill mused, "we'll see. If the end result is
10 weeping and wailing, we'll wish we had of taken less
11 kids. But Charlie Smith did the exact same trip last
12 summer and said it was fine. But he errored, though,
13 in taking his wife along. When they got back, she was
14 real beat!"

15   "Right," agreed Bob, "they sure came to a mutual
16 agreement that a bad trip is when any one person in
17 the crew is unhappy. She was literally livid when they
18 ended the week."

19   "Well, the issue is mute at this point in time. We
20 don't have this problem. Let's check the food sacks
21 again, irregardless of the fact that Martha's already
22 done it and make a list."

23   The cans and boxes were spread over the living
24 room floor. "How about stew?" Bob began. "Like I
25 always say, it makes a real big hit for dinner, and, if
26 you're hungry enough, it tastes like you'd of made a
27 Thanksgiving feast."

28   "You bet," was the reply. "We have a consensus
29 of opinion on that! There's times on a trip when I would
30 of swam a mile for a can of good beef stew. Let's see
31 — there's 23, 24, 25 cans in all. And a dozen smaller
32 cans make 37."

33   "I've checked all the cans and jars," said Bill, "and
34 none is leaking. I'm loathe to get to the bottom of a
35 back-pack and see that it needs washed and the
36 reason is because I was carrying around a leaker!"

37   "Right. I remember once soaking two pair of socks
38 on account of a lid was loose without me knowing
39 about it till too late."

40   "Good point," said Bill. "If I was you, I'd check the
41 lids to see that there's been none work loose."

42   "Right. Neither you or I want soupy socks!"

43   The next day was clear and sunny, and the gang
44 in the van set off in high spirits. The two dads and
45 three boys comprised the camping party. Since two
46 canoes would be used, the end result would be Bob,
47 with his sons Chuck and Hank, in one canoe, and Bill,
48 with his son Billy, in the other.

49   The van rolled quickly along the curvy country
50 road when Billy, as expected, spoke up. "Dad, can I
51 have some gum — I'm feeling a little nauseous."

52   "Well, o.k.," said Bill. "Here's a pack, and you and
53 Chuck split it among the both of you. Hank has some. If
54 I was you, I'd make that pack last — we have a ways to
55 go yet. And I can't hardly buy anymore out here."

56   Rolling along through the open country at 60 mile
57 an hour, the van ate up the miles.

58   "Hopefully, this road will get us to the camp by
59 3:00 P.M. this afternoon," said Bob.

60   "Irregardless of the time," replied Bill, "I'm in for a
61 swim in the stream when we get there." The boys
62 cheered.

63   Bob's prediction was correct, and they were soon
64 setting up camp.

65   "Bring those empty boxes back to the van over
66   there, boys," said Bill. "Now, in regards to a swim,
67   who's going in with me?" The boys let out a yell and
68   were only a step behind into the stream.

69   Floating around in a quiet pond at the campsite,
70   the boys were full of questions.

71   "In the spring, won't the water raise up and over-
72   flow the bank there?" Billy asked. "No," replied Bob,
73   "this type stream is wide enough so that won't hap-
74   pen." The usual thing for overflow is you have a
75   narrow stream and a big catch area — plus a lot of
76   rain, of course."

77   Later, around the campfire, the sleepy boys still
78   had a few questions. "Is there more logs of the kind
79   that pop and snap on the fire?" asked Chuck. "And
80   why do they pop?"

81   "There's a few more," said Bill. "The ones that
82   don't pop have less little beads of water trapped in the
83   wood, so less steam explosions."

84   Soon it was time for the sleeping bags. "Don't
85   anyone forget their mosquito spray before you lay
86   down," Bill reminded the gang. In minutes the kids
87   were asleep.

88   "This is the rare time of life where you can be real
89   close to your kids," Bob mused, as he wriggled into his
90   sleeping bag.

91   "You bet," said Bill, "and it's somewhat unique to
92   have these kids at the age where they all really enjoy
93   camping. Good night."

Answers

Line	Entry	Page
3	I/ME	47-48
4	GENTLER; OF	40, 73
5	OF/HAVE	74
6	EAGER/ANXIOUS	30
7	A.M./P.M.	1
9	END RESULT	32
10	OF/HAVE;	74
10	LESS/FEWER	59
11	EXACT SAME	35
12	ERROR/ERR	33
14	REAL/REALLY	94
14	BEATEN/BEAT	14
15	MUTUAL (AGREEMENT)	67
16	WHEN	73, 115
17	LITERALLY; LIVID	64, 64
19	MOOT/MUTE; POINT	148, 88
20	THIS	107
21	IRREGARDLESS	54
21	IT'S/IT HAS	55
24	LIKE/AS/AS IF	62
25	REAL/REALLY	94
26	LIKE/AS/AS IF	62
26	OF/HAVE	74
28	CONSENSUS	24
29	THERE IS/ARE	106
30	OF/HAVE	74
30	PAST PARTICIPLE	81
31	THERE IS/ARE	106
32	PLUS (MAKES)	87
34	NONE IS/ARE	71
34	LOATH/LOATHE	145
35	NEEDS (TO BE)	69
36	BECAUSE	15
37	PAIR/PAIRS	80
38	ON ACCOUNT OF	75
38	ING WORDS	51
40	SUBJUNCTIVE	102

CONTINUED